BY THE AUTHOR AND WAYNE WINTERROWD

A Year at North Hill:
Four Seasons in a Vermont Garden

Elements of
Garden Design

Joe Eck

Drawings by Lisa Brooks

An Owl Book

Henry Holt and Company • New York

Henry Holt and Company, Inc.
Publishers since 1866
115 West 18th Street
New York, New York 10011

Henry Holt® is a registered
trademark of Henry Holt and Company, Inc.

Published in Canada by Fitzhenry & Whiteside Ltd.,
195 Allstate Parkway, Markham, Ontario L3R 4T8.

Library of Congress Cataloging-in-Publication Data
Eck, Joe.
Elements of garden design/Joe Eck;
drawings by Lisa Brooks—1st ed.
p.   cm.
Includes index.
1. Gardens—Design.   2. Gardening.   I. Title.
SB473.E246   1996   95-235
712'.6—dc20   CIP

ISBN 0-8050-3719-5
ISBN 0-8050-5032-9 (An Owl Book: pbk.)

Henry Holt books are available for special promotions
and premiums. For details contact: Director, Special Markets.

First published in hardcover in 1996 by
Henry Holt and Company, Inc.

First Owl Book Edition—1997

Designed by Paula R. Szafranski

Printed in the United States of America
All first editions are printed on acid-free paper.∞

3   5   7   9   10   8   6   4   2
1   3   5   7   9   10   8   6   4   2
(pbk.)

For
Wayne Winterrowd

Acknowledgments

Pausing to remember whom one ought to thank for help in writing a book can call to mind a surprising lot of personal history. Nearest in this case would be Tom Cooper, esteemed editor of *Horticulture* magazine, who first suggested a series of pieces on garden design, offered the considerable talent and kindness of that publication's staff, and then for nearly three years featured the writings in the magazine. Next would be Tom Fisher, whose work as editor was in the old style—which is to say engaged with me in continuing dialogue about ideas and language, which immeasurably enriched and clarified what I was about. The series run, Ray Roberts, my editor at Holt, and Helen Pratt, agent and dear friend, pressed and encouraged me to gather them into a manual which might serve an even larger gardening public.

But beyond all these good friends who helped at close hand, I would have others to thank. Certainly Wayne Winterrowd, companion of my life and best colleague, whose sense of how gardens are made is now so much my own, or perhaps mine his, that there is no telling the difference. And I would thank parents who in the struggle to raise up many children never let them forget that ideas mattered, and their pursuit most of all. But last and best, I'd thank my grandmother Elizabeth McIver, long dead, who when told she must give up her gardening to lengthen her life, picked up her trowel and went to weed.

Contents

Introduction

New gardeners in search of guidance on how to make a garden will be surprised at how few books exist on the subject of garden design. There are many that discuss how to grow things—books on soil and compost, on pests and diseases, on trees and shrubs, on perennials, alpines, and vegetables. There are books about specific gardens—Sissinghurst and Great Dixter, Monticello and Middleton Place; and on great gardeners and garden makers—Gertrude Jekyll, William Robinson, Lawrence Johnson, Beatrix Farrand, Fletcher Steel, and Russell Page. There are books about color harmonies, plant growth rates, and pruning. A seemingly endless number exist on roses, but there are books on other genera and species, on geraniums, gentians, willows, poppies, daffodils, daylilies, and irises. Just lately, books have also appeared on "style," on cottage gardens, mixed borders, wildflower meadows, and on the contributions made by countries other than England—the gardens of France, of Italy, and of Japan. The effect of this groaning shelf of garden books is to provide the beginning gardener with a great deal of information, and—from photographic images and descriptions—considerable inspiration. By sifting and winnowing the greatest garden writers—Sackville-

West, Jekyll, Page, Robinson, and among those living now, Penelope Hobhouse, Beth Chatto, Christopher Lloyd, Rosemary Verey, Pam Harper—one can gather some precious hints on how gardens are made. But for those who like to proceed from first principles, who crave a certain order and coherence about thinking on any subject, there are very few books to turn to.

Probably many gardeners would consider that a good thing. That gardens are *designed,* that they reflect a series of choices, conscious or unconscious, successful or ill-considered, is for many gardeners a heretical—almost a repugnant—notion. Other human activities that hover between craft and art have leapt ahead in this; cooking, for example, is an activity in which instruction on principles and techniques is now quite fashionable, although it would once have been considered impertinent. In the garden, however, it is still assumed that one should do what one pleases, and that if one *is* pleased, that is all that matters. "Just remember," one perennial plant catalog recently remarked, "if you like it, it is *right.*"

Well, perhaps. But the argument of this book is that what defines a garden is less what is grown in it than how what grows is arranged. To be sure, it is always wonderful to see good plants in a garden, whether they are the latest rare import from Korea or China or a sturdy old lilac or rose passed from gardener to gardener for the last hundred years. Vigor and good health are necessary preconditions, for no garden can be really beautiful where the plants in it are not happy. But beyond that—or more accurately, *before* it—what pleases most in a garden is its design, the conscious thought and deliberate arrangement that gives it its quality.

Even the most casual of visitors to gardens recognizes that they are not all equal in beauty. So to ask—and answer—the question "Why is this garden beautiful, and that one less so?" is to be well along the way to making a beautiful garden oneself. And to ask that question of many beautiful gardens, and find that the answers are often the same, is to be well along the way to a theory of at least the essential preconditions for beauty in gardens. The purpose of such an aesthetic might be merely appreciatory, making us better tourists in other people's gardens. Certainly that would be a happy consequence of developing our ideas on garden beauty, but the principles we end up with will probably have their best and most valid application (in our eyes at least) right on our own patch of ground, right in our own garden.

This book is a codification of many perceptions and observations. Some have been gleaned from the wealth of beautiful picture books that have appeared in the last twenty years, which it has become fashionable to scorn as a sort of garden pornography, although I have been glad for every one that has been published. Other ideas—the best, most certainly—have come from the great garden writers of the past and present, whose works, though generally spontaneous, like good garden talk should be, are still generously sprinkled with observations about good garden design. Good gardening friends (some of whom are also writers, and some not) have offered, in conversation, treasures greater than they knew, the greatest of which is always that chance remark that causes one to say inside oneself, "Ha! *That's* it!" Even casual conversations, overheard in gardens open to the public, have helped to cause the coalescence of ideas which it is the purpose of this book to offer. Borrowed as it thus is, it would be both dishonest and rash of me to claim that there is much originality in it. Its primary value is one of convenience. And also—or so I hope—of provocation.

For, in part, this is a book of rules. Rules are both the life and death of any art. When fresh and new, they strike the interested as revelations; followed slavishly, they yield results that are sterile and formulaic. The end of the life of any rule, perhaps, is the creation of deep boredom, although along the way, if it had sense in it to begin with, it will have created other, healthier things. Genius can make do with almost anything—or nothing—to work its way; most of the rest of us do like a rule or two, to prop us up, to lean back on when we are tired. Or to argue with, when we ourselves grow bored and feel something like genius coming on.

Not every reader will give ready assent to every prescription laid down in this book, and for that I am grateful. Some rules are clearly more important than others. Those that define the very shape of the garden or its dominating emotional resonance are perhaps the ones I would be least willing to put aside, although there are good neighborly folks in parts of North America who do *not* want their gardens enclosed by a defining frame, and there are others—plant collectors, chiefly—who chafe against any clear intention for a garden simply because it would forbid them from growing a hardy cactus among their primroses. Let them then make their own rules, and let me dispute with them; for, in addition to being great fun, the colloquy will lead us some further way toward the creation of an aesthetic of gardens.

That, actually, is the main purpose of this book. One turns to any book for satisfaction, even if only for the satisfaction of laying it aside, five pages read, with the surety that one's taste, one's sense of things, is stronger than the author's. Obviously, I have somewhat higher hopes than that. I hope that new gardeners, just beginning to think about the shaping and configuring of garden space for enduring pleasure, will find perceptions within this book that will guide them in their choices and help them avoid costly and painful errors. It would be nice to suppose, also, that gardeners of some experience could find within these pages answers to questions that have baffled them, or a sentence or two that will coalesce a perception they have been on the edge of grasping for some time. The highest garden judges, if they turn to this book at all, must simply smile on it, and perhaps murmur a gentle "Yes, but, think of this also." All of these imagined responses—even the first of them—will further the essential aim of this book, which is, quite simply, to encourage a dialogue on how gardens are made.

Part I

Theory

Intention

Like all the arts, gardening must be guided by an intention. For many, that intention will be to recreate some other garden, one that seems, from childhood memory or adult experience, ideally beautiful. For others, nature will be the model, and the garden, on a smaller scale, will exist to remind them of a natural landscape—an alpine meadow, a field of wildflowers, or a shady woodland walk. But many of us, in making our gardens, are guided less by examples in the mind than by a simple passion for plants. And although all gardeners love plants, they love them for very different reasons, and so make their gardens from very different impulses.

Some gardeners want to be collectors; they are addicts given to the pleasure that comes from owning simply *all* of something—every variety in the species, every species in the genus, every genus in the family. Others are lovers of color, of rich masses of it crushed together in great romantic sweeps or shifting from shade to shade in subtle adumbration (yellow to yellow-ivory to rich cream to milk-white to chalk to . . .). Still others love plants for their perfume, endlessly varied and susceptible to minute discrimination, one from another. ("The smell of nutmeg," a great

3

nose once told me, "is really twelve distinct fragrances. Three of them are *not* pleasant.") And then there are botanists, whose interest lies in the infinite articulation of nature's order. ("It's a homely plant, to be sure, but it *is* the only member of its genus that is circumpolar.") Each of these intentions—and a thousand others—can result in the making of a beautiful garden, but only by acknowledging both the problems each poses and the solutions, successful or not, that other gardeners have attempted.

The problem posed by the collector's garden is one of sameness. Gardens composed chiefly of roses or lilacs, irises or daylilies or rhododendrons can fatigue even those who share the gardener's passion, for they are really but the vast multiplication of a single idea. Even the most beautiful gardens of this kind—Bagatelle, for example, with its roses or Keukenhof with its masses of tulips—can be reduced in the eyes of a demanding critic to bloom on bloom and yet more bloom. Public or private, they are what one might call "tourists' gardens," the beauty of which might be breathtaking to visitors at their peak, but hardly sustainable

throughout the growing year. They are only a step away from the growing fields, and there is neither quiet nor refreshment in them, because each garden unfolds all it has to offer at a single glance.

But the gardens of collectors need not reveal their intention at the first step we take into them. I know a garden of primitive plants, cycads chiefly, that still achieves in the dominant interest that governs it the qualities of variety and surprise. Its success lies in part in its terrain, a steeply sloping hillside threaded with paths and terraces that are hidden one from the other. But the gardener has also wisely varied his collection with other complementary plants—palms, aloes, and staghorn ferns—to create not just a sense of a primitive landscape, but also almost the *idea* of it, as if one were standing on the real bricks and looking at the real plants, transported into a landscape in the mind, a spot in the world—or its history—quite "someplace else."

The gardens of colorists face challenges of a different order. When one views a garden, the eye registers—often unconsciously—not merely color but also mass, volume, shape, and line. Gardens organized with an eye only to color, however successful its orchestration from shade to shade, often lack solidity even at the height of their season. One longs for a firm line, a satisfying neutral mass, an authoritative defining presence. And when not in flower, gardens that depend on color alone lack everything. It is for this reason that the carpet bedding still practiced in our large public parks is so unsatisfactory. One cannot look at such a plenitude of color without seeing the empty earth beneath. Conversely, the famous white garden at Sissinghurst is endlessly satisfying because it joins the finesse of its color scheme to the steady sustaining forces of yew hedge and green, trimmed boxwood and pavement.

The gardens of botanists, to give one last example, are concerned with scholarship. Their intention is the celebration of botanical or geographic relationships, sometimes to the minutest particular. At their worst, they can remind one rather forcefully of the dusty old-fashioned natural history museums to which one was taken as a child. They are not so much gardens as cases in which "specimens" are cataloged. If such plantings are to succeed as gardens, some larger and simply beautiful structure must embrace the botany. No better example of success in this regard exists than in Strybing Arboretum in San Francisco, where a defining frame of tall plants and trees surrounds the Arthur Menzies collection of native plants. A magnificent dry streambed structures it within, and a rondel of aged limestone defines its heart. The result is a satisfying picture during all seasons, even in the dead of winter and even to gardeners who may have no particular interest in the rich flora of California native plants.

A particular intention does not of itself yield a successful garden. One may have the clearest idea of what one *wishes* to create, but an idea—however necessary it may be as a starting point—still exists only in the mind. Its success will lie in its concrete realization, in the arrangement of treasured plants within a framework of less transitory elements, of trees, shrubs, hedges, pavement, architecture. Lucky is the gardener who begins with a clear intention, even though, as with all aesthetic impulses, it must be subject to endless adjustments, additions and deletions, delicate tamperings. Most of us, however, come to consider the dominant intention of our gardens rather late in our gardening life. ("I have begun to realize," a wise gardening friend once said to me, "that I have not actually made a garden. I have only made a nursery.") There is a point, after we have acquired our favorite plants and learned to grow them well, when we realize that the parts of our garden do not actually make up a whole. It is at that point that we begin to crave an intention, an idea that will make of the garden a unified whole, an aesthetic entity.

Fortunately, at that point, one need not go it alone. One can turn to memory, to the wisdom of other garden makers, to gardens one has lived in, or visited, or merely read about. For this much is certain: Gardening, like all the other arts, is not finally a private act. Whatever their personal passions—to collect, to gratify the sense of sight or smell, to study—gardeners are engaged in a colloquy, in a rich and complex conversation between garden and garden, gardener and gardener, living, dead, and yet to be born. The subject of that conversation is both the definition and the achievement of a beautiful and satisfying place.

Site

Of all the arts, perhaps painting and gardening are the most closely allied. Each is concerned with form and color and with the definition of space. Each is intended for the eyes. And much of the vocabulary appropriate to the one serves also for the other—color, mass, texture, volume, contrast, and so forth. But when one art is held against another, the most illuminating comparison is often the one that notes differences rather than similarities. Of all the differences that suggest themselves, none seems greater than the blank canvas with which the painter must begin, and the anything but blank site that confronts the gardener.

Both site and canvas are givens. But whereas the painter works on an essentially empty surface—or if he does not, at least *chooses* not to—the gardener works on a site that is already occupied. Further, the gardener is not the only maker of the garden. For from the first, the gardener shares the making of the garden with nature. And nature is often the more potent of the garden's two creators; sometimes it is its destroyer as well. The making of any successful garden, therefore, requires a congruence of the gardener's intentions and what the site will allow. Obvious although this fact may be, it is still useful to review the major limitations that considerations of site impose on the gardener's creativity.

First is the soil, which might be heavy or free-draining, rich or barren, deep or thin, acidic or alkaline. It is sometimes simple to alter the basic composition of the soil. A little lime, for example, can make acidic soils appropriate for the growth of most border perennials. Conversely, a thin soil can be amended by the addition of peat or humus. But, sometimes, the alteration of the soil is a daunting labor and a sure path to heartbreak. Usually the gardener will be far happier if he comes to love what his soil allows him to grow well, rather than willfully imposing on it plants that it can never support. On heavy clay, for example, he will do far better to nurture roses than to attempt the lightening and draining of the soil for high-mountain alpines. An acid, peaty soil might perfectly support a collection of rare heaths and heathers but be a dismal matrix for delphiniums and Oriental poppies.

As much as the soil, the climate of a garden radically affects its nature. The beautiful blue Himalayan poppy (*Meconopsis betonicifolia*), for example, will not grow on the humid mid-Atlantic coast, yet it flourishes in the cool hills of Vermont, a compensation for so much else that does not survive there. Camellias make winter gardening exciting in the Deep South, but would never survive the winter in USDA zones 3 and 4. And the lush herbaceous borders so many gardeners covet are practically impossible in arid Los Angeles, where the fascinating drought-tolerant flora of the Mediterranean coast and Australia, the beautiful, winter-flowering South African bulbs, are all perfectly at home.

The shape of the land—its topography—also controls the nature of the garden that lives upon it. Formal gardens require level terrain, since they depend on the regular planes of geometry for their effect. Where the land is hilly, a formal garden can be achieved only by artificially leveling and terracing the land. A garden of winding paths, of rustic steps up and down to follow the terrain, of woodland and spontaneous, seemingly wild plantings, would look far better on such a site. Similarly, a garden carved into little hills and valleys looks artificial when placed within an essentially flat landscape, where there are not greater hills and valleys to reflect its shape.

It is true that nature, up to a point, can, and often should, be compelled by the gardener. But the very best gardens are made when nature is a collaborator rather than an adversary. Often, that part of a gardener's site that seems at first a painful liability turns out in the end to be the very genius of the garden, its best asset. So the swampy area over which the gardener envisions yet more lawn, or perhaps a patch of roses or border perennials, *could* be drained and filled, with much labor and expense, and perhaps, in the end, limited success. But it could also be preserved and enriched just as it is, to provide a habitat for the many beautiful plants that might thrive in such a place. That bit of wet and squishy ground might provide the perfect home for candelabra primroses, Siberian and Japanese iris, for splendid "skunk cabbages" (*Lysichiton americanus* and *camtschatcensis*), for the outrageously large elephant ears of *Petasites japonicus* var. *giganteus,* for the tender bright gold of marsh marigolds in earliest spring. Such plants would flourish there, and are the despair of gardeners with ever so much emerald lawn and delphiniums in towered ranks.

   Hard though it might be for the gardener in possession of a new site to hear, the first thing to do when beginning a garden is to do nothing at all. Attend acutely to what is before you. Learn the fall of light and shade across your site (in both winter and summer), its wind patterns, the places where autumn leaves and snow gather or are swept away. Pay attention especially to how water—from rain or out of the ground— flows over, through, or around it, or stands in puddles. Come to know the site intimately, and perhaps to love it, or parts of it, just as it is. Only then will your site and the garden in your mind conspire together to yield a garden on earth worth the name.

Frame

In the language of gardening, the word *frame* is usually understood to mean any device that sets off some part of the garden for special notice or contemplation, such as a pair of gateposts, a gap in a hedge, or a "window" carved among the branches of trees that reveals a view of the distant hills. *Enclosure,* by contrast, refers to any structure—whether hedge, wall, fence, or line of trees—that defines the garden as a whole, marking it off from all that lies around or beyond it.

Clearly the terms are related, as both designate attempts to focus and guide the eye of the viewer as he surveys the garden; but of the two, I prefer *frame* because its etymology suggests a positive rather than a negative gesture, an opening rather than a closing of possibilities. In the Germanic languages from which the word evolved, frame meant variously "to benefit, to construct, to manage, to proceed or make progress, to go forward or contrive." In gardening, as well, frame suggests creativity rather than negation, a bringing in rather than a leaving out.

For gardeners of an earlier age, the concept of the frame was both practical and emotional. From Eden on, gardens have been places of refuge—worlds set apart, nature heightened or nature perfected, but first, nature *enclosed.* The world beyond the garden might be arid or barren, or dark, tangled, and inhabited with beasts. Alien bands with blue-painted faces might lurk there, hostile of intent. But within the garden, life was ordered and fertile, soft, and safe. Our word *garden* derives, in fact, from the Old High German word *gart,* an enclosure or safe place, and the etymology of the word is preserved in *kindergarten,* a safe place for children.

Although we do not face the same threats our ancestors did, frames in gardens can still perform a practical function. Few Americans live in climates as hostile as those in which the walled garden developed, but we still all need refuge—as much spiritual as actual—from the world beyond. The noise of traffic, the visual afflictions of power lines and filling stations, the happy but heedless enthusiasm of the neighbors' children, perhaps even the ill humor of the neighbors themselves, all are distractions that are best left beyond the garden wall. But even when these irritants do not exist, and there are only open fields and woods beyond, a garden still needs a frame. The love of enclosure may come to

us from the womb, or it may be the result of our ambiguous attitude toward our species, which causes us both to love and to need to be apart from the company of our fellows. However it is, we seem to crave a little world all our own, set off from the greater world we inhabit and from which we so often feel the need to retreat.

If a garden is considered to be merely a space in which plants are grown intentionally, then there can be gardens without frames. But such gardens will seem vaguely incomplete, like a book without a cover, or beads without a string, or—to offer the most obvious analogy—like a painting without the border of wood or metal that sets it off from the blankness of the wall beyond. The uncovered book, the unstrung beads, the unmounted painting, all might be valuable, and even beautiful, but they will seem to wait for the one thing that will organize them and give them the full force of coherence. So it is also with the garden that lacks a frame.

An actual wall is not the only way to set off a garden and provide it with a frame, although if your resources are ample and you live in the right place, a firm structure of brick or mortared stone or even stuccoed adobe may better suggest a world apart than any other device. Usually such walls look best in an urban setting, where the inert materials that fashion them are not discordant with the surrounding streets and the masonry of buildings. Even there, however, the somewhat unfriendly statement they make needs softening by vines and creepers and shrubs. A fence, a really sturdy fence built to last, can do as well as a wall, and is sometimes almost as costly. It, too, seems to look best in worlds where dwellings are thick and the terrain is reasonably level. And it, too, will need the gentling of vines and shrubs.

For those who live in rural areas or whose resources are more modest, a living frame of green may be more practical and more harmonious with the surroundings than either a wall or a fence. Hedges require more patience than money, but when they are well maintained and properly pruned (wider at the bottom than at the top) they can be very handsome. Like walls and fences, they can be fit into a narrow space, an important consideration when land is at a premium. But also like walls and fences, their rigid lines seem to require the softness of perennials or lesser shrubs planted at their feet.

Gardeners who have more land at their disposal, or who dislike the formality of a wall or fence or hedge, might well consider a frame of mixed shrubbery or a conifer border. The two are kindred concepts, differing essentially only in the fact that the mixed shrubbery is composed primarily of deciduous woody plants and the conifer border of evergreens. (Both, incidentally, can profit from the inclusion of elements from the other; a deciduous shrubbery gains winter interest and added privacy from the careful placement of a few evergreens, and the somewhat funereal effect of a conifer border is relieved by an occasional flowering shrub.) Both can have a depth of fifteen feet or even more, but they should always be wide enough to accommodate plantings staggered into layers and bays rather than arranged in a single line. (For then one has only a hedge that lacks the primary reason a hedge has for existing, which is uniformity.) The pockets and undulations that result from a well-planted shrubbery or conifer border offer wonderful places for bulbs and for groupings of perennials, preferably those that are handsome in both leaf and flower. Even a graceful little tree, a hawthorne or crab apple or *Magnolia stellata,* can be carefully placed in them for added height and interest. For gardeners as interested in growing a diversity of plants as in securing privacy and a sense of closure, such frames are the best of all options.

When placed at the garden's perimeter, walls, fences, hedges, and shrub or conifer borders will constitute its major frame. It is a paradox, however, that the more firmly the outer edges of a garden are marked off, the more necessary it is to construct secondary frames within; otherwise, the garden will seem like a playground or an outdoor basketball court. To hold our interest, a garden must contain turnings and surprises and small secret places. Secondary frames—small hedges, bends and swellings in the beds, or even the side of a well-placed shed or garage—can conceal a part of the garden from view and delight us even when we know perfectly well what lies behind.

Secondary frames can be effective on an even smaller scale. A stone sink or trough, for example, can frame a prized group of alpine plants; a pot can set off a collection of herbs or provide a way to keep the bold, tropical beauty of a canna in harmony with a temperate garden.

But whatever frame the gardener employs, it should never call undue attention to itself. Certainly it should be as handsome as can be, and so we more or less rule out chain-link fences, sheets of corrugated metal, or walls cunningly fashioned of discarded tires. But of whatever material, the frame is not the garden, any more than the frame of a painting is the painting or the cover of a book the book. It is only that which makes the garden possible, and crucial as it is, it is there only to contain and display the beauty within.

Style

*T*he growing of plants and the making of a garden are not necessarily the
same thing. Just as the paint arrayed on the painter's palette is not a painting, so plants simply growing in the earth, however lustily, are not a garden. To make a garden is first to shape a space, and then to arrange
within it all the elements that will make it cohere into some pattern or
another. Although many assume plants to be the most important of those
elements, they are not always, or chiefly, so. There can be gardens with
no plants in them at all, as at the famous Zen garden in Kyoto, Ryoan-ji,
which consists entirely of rocks and raked gravel. There, as everywhere,
it is the pattern that makes the garden.

Certainly there is no shortage of patterns for gardens. Gardening is one
of the oldest of the arts, and over the 4,000 years or more of its practice,
many patterns, or styles, have developed. Often these styles are national
in character, so strong in the arrangement of their elements that we can
recognize them as Islamic gardens, Japanese gardens, French and English
and (even) American ones. And sometimes there are gardens that criss-
cross among these styles, borrowing from here and there in so original a
way that we call them simply "personal gardens."

At the most elementary level, garden styles may be divided into formal and informal. The formal style is marked by geometric regularity and by symmetry, one shape answering another to create a sense of order, balance, and repose. In our own country, perhaps the most compelling examples of the formal style are at Williamsburg, Virginia, where trimmed box hedges, espaliered fruit trees, and mellow brick walls and paths combine to create a world of calm and tranquility. Pictures of Williamsburg gardens always show them packed with tulips and overhung with flowering trees, but so clear is the sense of style that the gardens are lovely even in the dead of winter.

In contrast to the formal style is the informal, which eschews symmetry in favor of irregularity. Here the garden is a reflection of nature—interpreted, heightened, or dressed, but recognizably nature still. It is this style that has dominated English and American gardening for a century and a half. Splendid examples of it are at Winterthur in Delaware

and at Strybing Arboretum in San Francisco. Grand as they are, their style and aims are shared by many an un-acred gardener throughout America. But it would be a mistake to assume that the informal style makes things easier. Those whose gardening urges are tempered by a fair amount of laziness would do better with a formal plan, for it is less likely to slip into a mess. In fact, as a garden style, the informal is no less trouble to achieve than the formal, and is probably more so.

Simply to divide gardens into two contrasting styles is, of course, a vast oversimplification. Always, the most interesting gardens are those that cross back and forth between the two. They are oxymorons in which formality blends with exuberance, straight lines with billowy masses. Thus, for example, at Wave Hill in the Bronx, the geometric beds in the conservatory garden are almost (but not quite) obscured by a lush profusion of flowers.

But whether gardens are formal or informal or inspired combinations of the two, none exists in a stylistic void. Every aesthetic decision is in part the product of influence. We see gardens we have liked and others we have not; we have noted effects that pleased us and others that seemed contrived. All that history of looking and judging, of liking and resisting, is what we bring to the making of a garden. The precise blend of conscious decision and inchoate memory, or the rational with the deeply felt, amounts to our own personal style. Everything is to be gained by knowing precisely *why* one likes this or that element of a garden, why one chooses this or that line or shape of bed or backdrop—in short, by knowing what effect one is aiming at.

That is simply to say that the more one looks at gardens, actually or in books, and the more one thinks about them and tries to isolate what is pleasing about them (or not), the better one's own garden is likely to be. Like any other art, gardening begins with borrowing. Where it goes from there determines whether the garden will be beautiful and satisfying or whether it will falter and fail to cohere.

S*tructure*

Nothing is as reassuring to the new or inexperienced gardener as a site plan. These drawings, with their little green circles for shrubs and their big ones for trees, with their clearly drawn bed lines and solid-seeming paths, carry an almost mystical authority. Yet one could hardly estimate how many garden failures result from following them.

Site plans effectively illustrate the structure of a garden viewed from overhead and flattened into two dimensions. Real gardens, on the other hand, rise up off the plane of the earth. They can be walked around, entered, and viewed from many angles (although almost never from above). They are more like sculptures than drawings, concerned much more with volume and mass than with color and line.

The act of gardening, too, is much like that of sculpting. A gardener often actually shapes the earth, hollowing it out, casting it up, making one space level and another contoured. But the ground is not the gardener's only medium. A gardener sculpts the air also, hollowing out of its insubstantial mass forms and structures. The gardener, of course, works the air by addition rather than subtraction, but the effect is the same—to organize space into a series of significant and interrelated forms.

In the language of garden design, the word *structure* designates all that is hard and bulks large. The structure of a garden is what is visible at a distance and what is seen in winter, when nature has stripped the garden of its flesh, leaving only bones on view. Then, without the distractions of color, scent, and sound, the form of the garden asserts itself. And it is the form of the garden that finally makes it pleasing or not.

The chief structural elements of a garden are its buildings; its walls, fences, and hedges; its paths, steps, stairs, and bridges; its terraces; and, not least, its woody plants. All these shape the garden by occupying space and by defining the open spaces between them. Over the centuries, much thought has been given to the proportions these structures should embody if they are to seem harmonious and pleasing. Mathematical formulas were developed, which, if followed, were believed to yield successful—that is, beautiful—spaces.

The most celebrated of these formulas is the one advanced by the thirteenth-century Italian mathematician Leonardo Fibonacci. It consists of a series of numbers beginning with 1 and 2. Each subsequent number of the series is the sum of the two that precede it (as 3, 5, 8, 13, 21, etc.). In determining the dimensions of an enclosed garden or terrace or the proportions of a summerhouse or arbor, Fibonacci's rule demands that one base one's measurements on adjacent numbers in the series. The authority of Fibonacci's work was enormously strengthened by the discovery that his mathematical series reflected the natural growth patterns of the vegetable and animal world, as is illustrated, for example, by the elegant shell of the chambered nautilus.

Modern theories of design have tended to emphasize a responsiveness to the environment over abstract mathematical calculations, stressing an awareness of the essential shape of the land, the vagaries of the climate, the local gardening tradition, and, most significantly, the uses of the garden space, the various functions it must accommodate. But blind adherence to any predetermined formula in the shaping of a space, although it may yield a well-proportioned garden, can also easily yield a lifeless one. More helpful than setting down unvarying rules of composition might be a look at the procedure by which a garden's structure is determined.

The first step in creating a garden is to establish firmly its outer limits, which, after the house itself, will be its most prominent and most important element of structure. One works from the edges inward, despite the fact that most new gardeners will be far more concerned with what lies closer to view than with what lies far away across the lawn. Still, a flower bed around the terrace is only a flower bed, not a garden, It is not even *part* of a garden if the garden's frame has yet to be determined, and, however pretty in itself, it may even be an indigestible distraction or an obstacle to future development. Tentative and spontaneous additions to a garden space can often become its most serious liabilities, especially when they are well-developed young trees or costly hedges of evergreens, for few gardeners have the ruthless courage to chain-saw them away or grub them up, even after it has become painfully apparent that they are in the wrong place.

Within the large, all-inclusive enclosure that is the garden's frame, smaller divisions into separate areas, or rooms, are made next. These should reflect the various activities that occur in any garden, from the most serious horticultural pursuits to the purely practical need of a place for the children to play or the dog to run. Once these rooms have been determined, a way to get from one to another must be provided. Although paths and walks are practical necessities, they are also major structural elements, almost as important in defining garden space as are walls and fences. And, of course, the placement of the larger trees and shrubs will also define separate garden spaces and determine the garden's eventual underlying character and plantings (bright-sunny, cool-shady, open spaces full of cheerful flowers or pensive green woodland walks, and so forth). Probably more heartache and disappointment have resulted from a failure to calculate the effects of the placement of major trees than from any other single cause. For unlike walls and paths, a tree is a living structure that will grow up (sometimes with surprising rapidity), spread out, cast shade, take moisture and nutrients to itself, alter the scale of the garden, and eventually die.

If planning on paper can lead the gardener to miscalculate, planning is itself still enormously useful. But the planning is best done in three dimensions. A box of damp sand, some sticks, twigs and sprigs of evergreen, some cardboard and perhaps a few pipe-cleaner figures for scale make it possible to fashion a garden in miniature, to try out endless combinations of elements. Working at this level, it is only the larger structural elements of a garden that can be manipulated, its sheds or outbuildings, its walls, hedges, or fences, its terraces and paths, its major shrubs and trees. That is all to the good, since it is these elements that are ultimately responsible for the success of the garden.

Rooms

One of the most significant ideas ever developed on the making of gardens is the concept of organizing them the way houses are, with separate rooms given over to different effects, purposes, or uses. Endlessly suggestive as that idea is, it is also rather obvious, as the best ideas tend to be once you have thought of them. And it is also very practical, for putting aside aesthetic and even spiritual issues for a moment, the chief value of organizing the garden into rooms is that it solves so many of the problems gardeners face, the first of which is perhaps the inborn urge to acquire.

One of the main pleasures of gardening is the growing of a great many plants, plants of all sizes, shapes, colors, and seasons of bloom. But if these plants are all to lie down together serenely and harmoniously, without conflict or discord, some way must be found, first, to sort them out into sympathetic communities, and second, to create a feeling of unity among these communities.

We sort our plants first by their own cultural preferences—sun lovers with sun lovers, shade plants in the shade, plants that crave a peaty, acid duff in one part of the garden and those that demand a sweet, alkaline loam in another. Not only do plants so arranged grow better, they *look* better, too, according to a law that declares a harmony between plants that originated in the same natural conditions, and a discord between those that originated in disparate ones.

We may also sort our plants by season of bloom—spring flowers in one part of the garden, those of high summer in another. Seasonal sorting not only allows us to concentrate the maximum amount of flower in one space, but it also allows us to avoid grouping plants together, some of which will look their worst just as their neighbors are reaching perfection. And we might also want to arrange our plants by color harmonies, sequestering all the hot oranges and reds from the misty blues, pinks, and mauves. Perhaps we dream of contriving gardens all of one color, such as the famous red border at Hidcote or the sublime white garden at Sissinghurst.

It is not easy—it may not even be possible—to separate a garden into areas for different kinds of plants or effects without some way of screening off one area from another. And even if one could achieve such separation without the use of hedges, walls, fences, buildings, or masses of tall shrubbery, the garden would lie all before one, apparent at a single glance. It would thus sacrifice the second great value of the concept of rooms, the delight of surprise.

On its surface, the concept of dividing the garden into rooms seems most applicable to quite large gardens, where ample terraces give way to extensive, hedged perennial borders or to a formal rose garden, and from there, across a generous lawn to plantings of ornamental shrubs screening a pool or facing down a woodland edge. But the concept of rooms is equally applicable to quite small gardens, where it is possible, and desirable, to set aside a corner for a shaded bench, a small, quiet pool, or a tiny, orderly plot for herbs and salad greens. And the garden, small though it may be, will seem to become larger by offering a greater diversity of experience.

On a very rudimentary level, separate rooms already exist on most American properties. The house itself divides the property into a front yard, a backyard, and one or two side yards. Service areas for raked leaves and trash cans are usually walled off in some way. Vegetable gardens are almost always set apart by fencing or hedging, and are, because they are screened, often the most interesting parts of the property. But what does not generally occur in America is the division of the purely ornamental parts of the garden into rooms.

Like any other aspect of gardening, garden rooms can be divided into those that reflect formal or informal intent. Formal rooms are usually rectilinear in shape, although sometimes round or oval, and are strictly defined in some way, usually by hedges or walls. Rooms of this formal sort, unless very large, require level ground. Where there is space, sloping ground may be terraced, but never at the expense of the tranquility such spaces demand, for a certain clear expansiveness is their essence. In the informal landscape, rooms might be defined by loose bays of shrubbery, by trees and ground covers, or even by berms of earth. In very small gardens, sometimes a single large evergreen around which a path curves, or a grouping of lilacs or rhododendrons, is enough to separate one area from another, partially masking and giving mystery to what lies beyond. But whether formal or informal, what is essential about a garden room is that it both feel and be separate from what lies around it. Each room should seem to form a world entire unto itself, a retreat from distraction

even when that distraction is other equally compelling parts of the garden. In any garden room, one should feel the need to remain for a while, to rest and see before going forward.

So, in early spring, in what New Englanders so descriptively call mud season, a room could be set apart for all the little bulbs, welcome after the long winter but hardly looking their best near still-brown grass and sodden piles of leaves. Later, in summer, such a room might display ferns or hostas, or later still, the September-and-October blooming *Cyclamen hederifolium.*

Sometimes plants we couldn't think of being without because they are so beautiful in their season have little to offer at other times, or worse, become positive liabilities for the overall beauty of the garden. Bearded irises, for example, are one of early summer's great displays, but by August, they are disfigured by heat, humidity, and fungus. Grown all massed together in their own space, they offer the best they have to give, becoming the garden's most important part when they are in their moment of glory, and a part easily overlooked when they have grown sad and tired. Like so many plants that offer endless variety within an overall similarity of form, a room given over to them alone is often loveliest when it is rather long and narrow, a sort of walk along which one can stroll to admire the many separate changes on a single theme. So a neglected strip of earth along a garage wall or a sunny, narrow side yard might be the perfect place for an "iris room" or—if such a spot is shady—for a fascinating collection of hostas or ferns.

Many plants with particular and exacting cultural requirements can be accommodated, and set off to advantage, by being given their own space in the garden, their own garden room. Choice alpines, for example, need open soil, bright light, and freedom from the competition of trees and shrubs. And their high-mountain diminutiveness makes them easily lost in a general planting of larger perennials and bolder flowering plants. Rockeries, at least as most American gardeners seem to employ them, can be disasters in the landscape, chiefly because they are unconvincingly built in full view, along the front of the house or in the middle of a sweep of lawn. But a few handsome rocks, buried at least a third their depth in the earth in a separate and hidden part of the garden, can provide both the perfect home for tiny alpine plants and a delightful surprise in the garden.

Perhaps the greatest merit of a garden organized as a series of separate rooms is the pleasure it gives when one passes from here to there. Such gardens, whatever their size, cannot be seen all at once but must be sought out and discovered, part by part. Behind a hedge there may be treasures that have appeared in the night, new spring shoots that have pierced the earth, or long-hoped-for buds at last unfurled. Surprises, what garden connoisseurs call "events," are always waiting. No matter how well one knows one's garden, one never knows.

A̧ccess

*O*f the many delights a garden can offer, one of the most precious occurs when it cannot be taken in all at a glance. Whether small or large, gardens that unfold slowly, that move from one hidden group of plants to another, from room to room or from light to shade and back to light again, mirror a little the infinite richness of nature itself. But gardens are not made by nature, who is only accidentally concerned with surprise and variety, with easy movement into and through space, and who would, if she could, thicken every foot of arable ground with impenetrable, uniform vegetation. It is the gardener who makes the garden, and who thereby gives access to his own private idea of the natural world. Although made cunningly of nature's elements, that idea must always owe its essential identity to the gardener's contrivance, to art.

More than any other element of garden design, it is access—the way we move into, about, and through a garden—that most bespeaks the gardener's personal vision of nature. Although metaphors drawn from painting or sculpture often suit other aspects of gardening, it is a comparison with literature—specifically with the novel—that most quickly illuminates the concept of access. For the way we are enticed into a garden and encouraged to pursue its experience to the end is like the plot of a novel. It is the thread on which the whole story unfolds.

Like the novelist, the gardener has the power to induce a surprising range of emotions. He may encourage simple delight, wonder, awe, excitement, or pleasurable surprise. But equally possible behind the garden gate are emotions more startling and less immediately gratifying, such as anxiety, confusion, claustrophobia, or even a faint sense of panic, as, for example, when we are lost in a garden maze. Any of these responses can be evoked, and can be made to play one against the other, as when a broad expanse of lawn, always intrinsically reassuring, is fringed with an impenetrable and mysterious wall of shrubbery, or when a path up a steep hill issues into a restful level glade, with perhaps a bench to reward us for the effort of the ascent.

To pursue the analogy of the garden and the novel, the garden's gates and entrances may be compared to a novel's title and chapter headings, and they may announce the experience of the garden honestly and directly or with a sense of irony. They often, but not always, signal its theme. A single stone pillar, for example, might mark the entrance to a country garden where the paths are made of flat fieldstone and the walls of old granite. A fresh, white-painted picket gate in a fence or hedge could signal the approach to an old-fashioned cottage garden, reassuringly trim and familiar, crowded with the flowers one remembers from childhood. Or, for irony, a magnificent pair of yews, trimmed into formal cones or perhaps into fanciful topiary birds and beasts, could flank the entrance to a meadow garden where all else is wild and seemingly spontaneous.

When one considers access in the garden, one is concerned primarily with walks and paths. They can be obvious, straight as an arrow, or very gently curved, leading without confusion to the front door or to an important feature of the property such as a swimming pool. They may be broad and level or terraced into gentle steps for easy ascent, allowing two or three people to walk together in sociable conversation. Or they can be so narrow as to allow the passage of only one person at a time, forcing attention onto the path itself and the plants that press against it. They can meander, curving around some obstacle such as a group of trees or a

large shrub, always tempting one on to see what lies beyond and forcing a leisured, desultory amble among the bushes. Most significantly, they can lead not only to, but *into* the garden, since a garden one can wander through is always more thrilling than a garden one must simply stand before and stare at.

As with all garden matters, effect should follow intent. So, where one wants direct and easy movement, the path surface should be smooth and uniform, perhaps of broad slabs of bluestone or well-packed gravel. A path of this kind should be generously wide, with its end clearly in view. Conversely, where the intent is to slow passage and encourage contemplation, the path might be narrow and contrived of materials that call attention to themselves, such as antique brick or weathered fieldstone laid in a beautiful but seemingly random pattern. Such lesser paths, the ones we travel not just to get from here to there but to see, lend themselves also to the precious garden value of contrast. If the path can be contrived so that a sunny border is followed by woodland or by shady copses of tall shrubs, or a dry bank on one side falls to a moist fecund bog on the other, it becomes not just a walkabout but an exploration of contrasting environments and habitats, each lending added value to the other. Such paths can also bring the gardener into richer association with parts of the garden he might not otherwise be able to observe closely. A fieldstone walk could give way to a wide bridge of weathered wood across a bog or over a garden pool; or it could broaden in a dry, sunny spot to accommodate tiny rock garden plants among the pavers.

All this may imply a good bit more control than most devoted gardeners can exercise over their own particular plot, great or small. And here the analogy to the novel becomes richest, for novelists who aim to tell a complicated story must know the moment when their characters take control of the plot and begin to unwind their destinies on their own. Time and again, we have all been thrilled to see the way a space or a collection of plants assumes its own life and begins to tell its own story, asking of us only a little help. Everything is gained when we begin to read these stories, to note their intent and effect, or more to the point, to note those intents and effects that almost work but don't quite, only for the want of a little more shade, a little more sun, the need for a path that acknowledges the daily trip we make to a favorite spot, or one that curves meaninglessly when it should go straight, or goes straight when a curve would add everything. Our best guides are often not our minds but our feet, which often, in unconscious routine or in seemingly aimless twilight rambles, show us the way to go.

H*armony*

The late Lester Hawkins, a distinguished plantsman, once remarked that in gardening the great art was "getting the plants to lie down together." Gardens are, after all, strikingly heterogeneous in all their parts. The plants themselves are drawn not only from the fields and woods that lie about, but also from far places—from Japan and China, England and Italy, Morocco and South Africa—that is, from the whole of the world. And they are taken from every possible habitat—alpine tundra, lowland bog, acid woodland, and alkaline shore. From the great trees that tower above to minute tuffets best viewed through a lens, they present every form imaginable. And to all this diverse wealth of plants, we add stone, brick, pools, and pergolas, and then ourselves, our dwellings, our animals, the rhythms of our daily lives. All we ask of this assembly of diverse elements is that it cohere so seamlessly that one cannot imagine it in any other way. This is harmony, and it is at once the most difficult and the most essential of the gardener's many arts.

Harmony is easiest to achieve when the scope of the garden is limited to plants native to the place. Such gardens can be deeply satisfying, as they achieve their congruence not only within themselves, but also with the world that lies beyond the garden, for both are compounded of the same elements. Even so, the natural garden, like any other, must be held together by strong and reassuring structures, by paths that give logical and easy access within, and by frames that both separate and blend the garden with its surroundings. For even the most natural-seeming gardens consist of plants that are grouped together, and they must always be grouped *against* something.

Of course, not all gardeners wish to grow only native plants, or are lucky enough to garden in places where nature lies beautifully all around. Some garden in places where nature has ceased to exist. Some want to make different kinds of gardens, gardens that are filled with exotic plants or that reflect other times, other places than the one the gardener is given to inhabit. For such gardeners, the first task is to arrange their plants so that they will seem content in each other's company, conveying the sense of inevitability that is always the underlying quality of a great garden, large or small.

The first requirement in achieving harmony in the garden (so obvious perhaps as to demand little comment) is to culture plants well, for a thriftless and miserable plant can never suggest the sense of repose on which harmony depends. Good health in plants requires the gardener's keen sense of their needs and a lot of hard work. But it also often requires that plants be grouped together according to their cultural preferences. So those that love sun and a limy soil, for example, are grown with others of their kind, and conversely, dryland plants are not asked to live by the side of those that originate in wet meadows.

Many plants are inflexible in their cultural needs and will never flourish when their preferences are violated. Others seem endlessly compliant and adaptive, but even these carry with them a memory, sometimes more aesthetic than actual, of the conditions in which they originated. So, in a brash and highly colored herbaceous border, hostas might grow perfectly well in the shadows of taller companions. But they will always carry a sense of lush woodland and might look far better with astilbes and ferns than with coreopsis and gallardias. *Kirengeshoma palmata*, an elegant perennial native to the woods of Kyushu, Japan, will endure the full light of the sun if it is kept sufficiently moist; but it would look odd and out of place next to border phlox, and it would lose by such a placement much of its wonderful

beauty. Marigolds might be made to flourish at the feet of rhododendrons, for they seem able to flourish almost anywhere. But one would not like to see them associated with such companions. It simply wouldn't do.

Even careful siting of plants according to their cultural needs, and keeping them segregated from other plants whose needs are different, may not result in harmony. For in every garden there are plants that might flourish, but that must be ruled out simply because they convey qualities that are too deeply at variance with the world of that particular garden. Cacti, for example (and particularly Opuntias, the "prickly pears") are native to some surprisingly cold places in North America. They can be made to grow in hilly, zone 4 gardens in Vermont; I know, for I have grown them. But they always seemed anomalous and faintly embarrassed in company with daffodils and hardy geraniums and antique shrub roses. No trick of framing or segregating them ever seemed successful, however well they thrived, in bringing them into harmony with their lush and luxuriant surroundings.

As important as the way we group plants is the way we shape them. Although gardening is often assumed to bring the gardener close to nature, plants are almost never successful in gardens when they are allowed to go entirely their own way. The hand of the gardener is on them almost from the first, no less in informal or "wild" gardens than in formal ones. Yews are harmonious elements in a formal garden when clipped into geometric shapes; they may be equally harmonious in a woodland garden, although there they still must be carefully pruned and shaped to reveal their handsome trunks and branches and to achieve an open, airy grace in harmony with the forest canopy. In shaping any plant, the goal of harmony requires that the gardener respect the innate character of a plant, assisting it to reveal what it is best for in the situation in which it is grown. Although yews may go either way, some plants will always look violated, and cruelly controlled, if they are asked to assume shapes not natural to them. The shearing of forsythia into a hard-edged, geometric shape, for example, is a violation of the plant's nature that nearly always results in a visually indigestible blob of yellow in the spring landscape. Conversely, a forsythia planted in light, dappled woodland shade will have fewer flowers, but greater grace, all of which, by subtraction, is gain. Still, however, even a forsythia must be controlled, by the removal of old and congested stems, to bring it into greater sympathy with the shimmering light around it.

The issue of harmony depends not only on the provenance of the plants and on the appropriateness with which they are combined, but also on the way they are arranged, one against another. We all know of gardens in which the virtue of tidiness is carried to such extremes that each plant is forbidden to touch its neighbor. Each is only itself, displayed as in a shop window or nursery yard. The community of a garden, the way one plant leans on its neighbor for support or borrows from it for visual effect, is denied, usually by a sea of wood chips marking off the space between plant and plant. Many of us, perhaps most of us, start off that way. It is not a bad start, for by segregating each plant into its own tidy space and growing it well, we come to know its special character, its beauty not only of flower but of leaf and stem. But at a certain point, we begin to realize that a collection of plants is only a collection of plants, a nursery, not a garden. It is the dependence of one plant on another, and the knitting together of so many distinct individuals into a harmonious whole greater than the sum of its parts, that makes a garden a garden. For gardens are peaceable kingdoms and gardeners are enlightened monarchs, enforcing order and tranquility, causing plants "to lie down together." The result is harmony.

Contrast

*T*he great problem with rules is that once they are laid down, people tend to observe them. So having argued, I hope persuasively, for the importance of making gardens that are harmonious and of a piece, I worry that a plague of sameness might be the result. Surely too much harmony is as fatal to beauty as too little.

A small story might underscore this point. A great English plantsman was once called in to evaluate a perennial garden which, for reasons mysterious to the owner, was vaguely displeasing to her. She had taken care to secure the best plants and had attended scrupulously to color harmonies. Maintenance was just as it should be. Still, the composition failed to satisfy. After strolling through the garden, admiring the fine plants there and the horticultural skill that had brought them to perfection, the plantsman's verdict was swift and sure. "Your leaves are all the same size."

Once the rule of harmony has been observed, the gardener's next concern is to skew it here and there, always tactfully, by the introduction of a little something else. Through the use of contrast, we secure the refreshment of variety while underscoring the predominant mood or texture of the garden. In other words, we double our values.

Virtually every garden element suggests its own foil. So, small leaves are contrasted to larger ones, the broad against the finely dissected. Plants that grow in low mats are juxtaposed to those that grow upright in clumps, and soft flower shades are given life by a dash of harder color. Horizontal masses, sometimes composed of many plants, demand the exclamation point of a strong vertical accent, be it an evergreen, a shrub pruned as a standard, or a weathered wooden post on which a vine has been trained.

The difficulty in employing contrast lies not so much in identifying its need as in introducing elements which, while providing a note of accent, are not overly incongruous or eccentric. Like so many issues in garden design, the contrasting elements selected depend on the personal taste or vision of the gardener. Still, some guidelines for the use of contrast can be offered.

The first is that contrasting elements ought to possess some degree of kinship with what lies around them, whether of leaf texture, shape, or even a strong preference for the same growing conditions. So, in a border given over to heaths and heathers, for example, the pronounced shapes of dwarf conifers might be introduced for contrast. Although they may grow rigidly upward or into formal rounded masses, their fine needles are similar in texture to heaths and heathers. High bush blueberries might provide an even bolder note of contrast, for although their growth habit and leaf texture are very different from those of heaths and heathers, their foliage, especially in autumn, burnishes to similar golds and reds. Both blueberries and conifers also share a preference with heaths and heathers for the thin, acid soils of the upland moors, and so they seem to consort well together by ancient association.

In a shady woodland garden, contrast might be achieved by setting large-leaved hostas or perhaps the dark-green, borage-leaved *Trachystemon orientalis* against the lacy foliage of maidenhair ferns or the cool-green fringe of *Dicentra eximia*. Beyond the fact that all these plants revel in cool woodland soils, they assume, for all their contrast in texture, mounded shapes that are similar in height and general outline.

Most large perennial borders suffer from a rather undifferentiated texture, since many of the plants we depend on for abundant flower color are similar in shape and fairly undistinguished in leaf. For this reason, the

splendid leathery foliage of peonies has always been valued as an excellent contrast, even when the flowers are long past. Lately, too, we have
learned to introduce tall grasses into the border, particularly species and
cultivars of *Miscanthus,* which offer contrast of shape, texture, and, in
some of the variegated forms, color. But in the perennial border, contrast
may be introduced with a somewhat bolder hand than elsewhere. Here
the rigidly conical shapes but soft, needled textures of some evergreens,
particularly the Alberta spruce (*Picea glauca* var. *albertiana*), might form a

satisfying foil to many lax perennials. Conversely, however, the beautiful Hinoki cypress (*Chamaecyparis obtusa*) might seem too redolent of the Japanese gardens in which it is so often planted.

Flower color can, of course, also be used for contrast in the perennial garden, and many a soft misty mauve and pink planting scheme would benefit by a dash of yellow. But it must be the *right* yellow, for although a drift of *Coreopsis verticillata* 'Moonbeam' can add vitality to a planting of pale blue and pink *Campanula lactiflora,* and even soften the assertive old rose of *Sidalcea malviflora,* the hard chrome yellow of *Coreopsis verticillata* 'Zagreb' would set everything at odds.

Color contrasts ought not to be thought of only in flowers, however, for leaves, too, can provide valuable color accents in the perennial garden. One thinks first of the value of silver, for there is no perennial garden, whether planted with hot oranges, yellows, and reds or soft blues, pinks, and mauves, that does not benefit from a generous admixture of silver leaves. Gold, too, although it is generally harder to come by than silver, is invaluable. Many an insipid planting of perennials might turn magical with a splash of canary-yellow foliage, from *Tanacetum parthenium* 'Aureum', for example, or from the introduction of one of several prunable shrubs such as the golden elder. And finally, purple, if it is used with great discretion (to avoid the "mournful widow" look) can provide an accent that makes everything around it look better. Clumps of the annual *Perilla frutescens,* or the perennial *Lysimachia ciliata,* or even shrubby purple-leaved berberis (*B. thunbergii* 'Atropurpurea' or 'Rosy Glow') can spark an otherwise dull perennial planting.

Inanimate objects can also provide contrast to growing plants. Stone is especially useful, whether it is an upright marker stone at the entrance to a woodland walk or a bit of carved architectural detail half lost in a bed of ferns. In country gardens, weathered wood is always wonderful as a sturdy corset for an old shrub rose or as a pillar on which to train honeysuckle, clematis, climbing roses, or annual vines. And nothing gives quite the same value in a garden as a fine, weathered clay pot, an old stone sink, or a lead urn, set for accent in a strategic place to show off a rare plant or even a tumble of annuals.

But it is with the use of inanimate objects as accents in the garden that the most important rule of contrast emerges. Nothing that is used for contrast in a garden ought ever to call so much attention to itself that it distracts from the whole. Elements of contrast must always be used with restraint. They are the spice to the dish, but no one would want to dine on cinnamon.

$Scale$

Gardens exist within the context of what is not garden. They are bounded on all sides by other entities, both man-made and natural. If they are urban gardens, they are surrounded by buildings; if rural, they exist in the center of a forest or a field. Above all gardens lies a vast sky, and in the hearts of most sit a house and perhaps other buildings as well. All these facts, taken together, determine a garden's scale, that is, the size of the garden itself and the elements that compose it.

Many gardens in America fail because they are too meager. They offer no effective balance to the mass of wood or masonry represented by a house that might be sixty or eighty feet in length, half again as wide, and thirty feet or more in height. Such gardens seem mere afterthoughts, as in fact they often are—obligatory side-dressings to more essential domestic concerns or perfunctory gestures at keeping up the standards of the neighborhood. Yet the beauty of a garden depends always on its seeming at one with the house, as essential to the life lived in that place as is the living room or dining room or kitchen, and often as ample, in size and in furnishings—and in the various uses to which parts of it may be put—as what lies withindoors.

The house that sits in the center of a garden is one of the two principal factors that determines its scale. The other is what lies beyond, be it adjacent buildings or nature itself. In an urban or suburban garden, it is other houses, usually, that dominate the garden's perimeter, but it may be public spaces, a school, a place of worship, or shops and office buildings. Such bounding structures may press too close to allow space for a garden to spread generously around the house at its center. In these cases it is always important to draw the eye upward at the garden's edge, perhaps by the use of a tall, narrow conifer or a group of them, a grove of upright flowering trees, or even a vine-clad fence, wall, or arbor. In this way the garden compensates in the vertical for what it lacks in the horizontal, and the distracting elements beyond that reminding us of the garden's limits are partially or completely concealed. Alternately, a confined urban garden can be made to seem larger by being self-consciously limited to miniature plants, to a whole tiny world of alpines and dwarf conifers so strong in character as to suggest a unique habitat. Although Japanese garden makers are preeminent in the practice of this sort of trompe l'oeil, a garden so constructed need not seem "Japanese" in its style; it could as easily reflect an eastern American woodland in miniature, or a dry California streambed, or the top of Mount Washington.

On rural properties the problem of scale is often much easier to solve, for there is usually sufficient space for the garden to spread amply around the house, reflecting—by terraces and by swards of mown grass, and even by separate "rooms"—the dimensions of its domestic center. On rural properties, also, there is usually the possibility of creating a frame for the garden, far enough from the house yet tall and dense enough to balance it. A frame of this kind has the ability to blend with the towering trees of the forest or to stop the eye from wandering restlessly over the fields.

Scale is, of course, as important within the garden as it is in controlling the garden's perimeter. The typical American "flower bed" is often a narrow strip two feet or so wide, backed by a six-foot-tall fence or dribbled along the foundation of a tall house. Almost always such plantings, no matter how choice the specimens may be within them or how well-tended, suffer from an appearance of stinginess. Although all good gardeners eventually come to be suspicious of ironclad rules, it is still a useful rule of thumb that

borders should extend in width at least two thirds the height of the structures that back them. In the case of foundation plantings, beds should be at least as wide as the largest plants in them are tall. Where space does not allow such extension, as, for example, between a house wall and a terrace, it is often necessary to limit the height of the plantings to achieve a greater illusion of space, or to extend them dramatically upward with a rhythmic sequence of rigid conifers or muscular deciduous shrubs or small trees, or perhaps with espaliers or trained vines, to create a second wall of green.

The most difficult problems of scale usually occur when some element within or adjacent to the garden looms above it, seeming to intimidate the garden space and the gardener alike. Such an element could be the house itself, a barn, a great deciduous tree, the stark "bean poles" of conifers surrounding a property newly reclaimed from the forest, or a structure on a neighbor's plot. In the case of trees, whether as isolated specimens or along the verges of the surrounding woods, sometimes the chain saw is the only answer. Gardeners tend to be very sentimental about trees, shuddering at the finality of eliminating a life that may be as long, or far longer, than theirs. Once the deed is done, however, the gain in light, and the increased possibilities for gardening, usually offer tremendous compensations for what is gone. And the removal of a vast Norway maple dwarfing a modest house will make possible the planting, in its place, of a smaller tree, more appropriate in scale and of more refined interest.

Sometimes, however, elements that are discordant in scale are givens that cannot be removed, and so they must be manipulated. No more useful lesson in their treatment exists than in the understory of much of the New England woodland, where a feathering of youthful trees or shrubs that love the shade cluster beneath the stark and towering gray boles of the mature forest. The principle that makes such woodland beautiful can be applied in a garden wherever any fixed element seems to overpower its surroundings by placing beneath it some other element that will seem to cut it in half and draw it down to earth. For example, a deciduous magnolia capable of achieving twenty feet at maturity could be placed at the corner of a high-shouldered Victorian house. In similar fashion, shadblows, dogwoods, native witch hazels, and rhododendrons could be grouped beneath or among trees that seem over-tall. Garden structures, also, can reflect the principle of understory, and so a greenhouse, a woodshed, or an old-fashioned grape arbor could tie to earth a stark house wall or a massive old barn.

Although occasionally problems in scale will force gardeners to think small, it is much more frequently the case that they force on them an amplitude of vision. Most often, solutions in problems of scale require that a bed be enlarged way beyond what was originally thought possible, that a hefty multitrunked crab apple be substituted for the smug pilled yew at the corner of the house, or that a broad terrace be laid outside the kitchen door. With scale, perhaps more than with any other principle of garden design, what is required of the gardener is often a certain degree of courage.

Mass

Not all plants contribute equally to the garden. We all grow plants whose loss we would mourn, but even when they depart, due to inadequate culture or a lack of suitability to their site, the garden remains. There are some plants, however, that are so essential to the structure of the garden that the gaps their demise leaves behind subtract materially from the beauty of the whole. Such plants are usually ones whose mass creates the very shape of the garden, dividing it into separate areas, providing a quiet backdrop against which its exuberance of flower or of foliage is arranged, making it a world apart. Mass is the expanse or bulk of a plant, the weight or space it occupies, its assertiveness, quiet or pronounced, in the landscape.

Of course, all plants occupy space. But some do so in far more authoritative ways than others. Plants that are dense have more mass than those that are airy. So a deciduous magnolia, both in leaf and in bare trunk and branch, is far more assertive in the garden than a shadblow. Spruces possess more mass than pines, for although the juvenile shape of both may be similar, the congested growth of a spruce stops the eye, whereas the loose growth of a pine invites it inward and beyond. Color, too, contributes to a feeling of mass. Dark plants absorb more light than pale ones and so seem heavier and more massive. Purple trees weigh more than green ones, a fact never more apparent than when a brooding purple beech is planted against the green-leaved form. The almost black-green of yews appears weightier than the yellow-green of arborvitaes. And obviously, deciduous plants, however massive in leaf, are much less so when autumn has stripped them of their foliage. The only exception are those plants so densely twiggy or so muscular in branch and limb that,

even when naked, they command their space. And large plants are more massive than smaller ones. Forest trees, even in winter, possess great weight and structural dignity just because their boles and primary limbs are so large. But lesser plants, slight of twig and stem, will always create in winter the faint sense of something missing.

In designing a garden, a consideration of mass is important in three ways. First, plants of significant mass define space. Whether grouped loosely in drifts or arranged in hedges, massive plants are essential in organizing the garden into areas or rooms, and in screening it from what lies around. And since the definition they provide is as necessary in winter as in summer—or more so—we tend to rely on evergreens to perform this crucial function.

Second, just as plants that carry significant mass create the larger structures of a garden, so also do they establish a rhythm within it. Each unit or room may itself be broken into a series of related units, called bays, or, to use a musical analogy, movements. What ties these disparate sections of the garden together is the repeated, rhythmic use of heavy but recessive elements beneath them. These repeated marks, sometimes of the same plant, sometimes of many that possess similar mass and density, control the way in which we see the garden at all seasons. They both segregate our gaze into separate events of perception and also subtly weld those perceptions into a satisfying whole. It is this sublime articulation of part to whole that creates a beautiful garden, whatever its scope.

Finally, mass may also be used to anchor the gardener's invention by means of a fixed, repeated pattern on the ground. This pattern may be symmetrical or asymmetrical in nature, the dark masses set at regular or irregular intervals throughout the garden. But it is just this solid bass line that holds the garden together, that keeps it from slipping into a wild and chaotic series of elaborations. Plants with significant mass, although they seldom or never are vivid with flower—and indeed, to fulfill their essential functions, ought not to be—provide resting places for the eye, to which it will return, as a bird to a satisfactory perch, after its flight through the garden.

In all but the most formal gardens, the underlying structures provided by plants that possess mass are recessive, not so much apparent in them-

selves as in what they make possible. Another analogy drawn from music
may clarify this point. Plants that possess mass function in a way similar
to the ground bass used in much baroque music. There, a sequence of
low sounds is arranged into a simple four- or eight-note pattern that is
repeated throughout the work. Above it the composer contrives fanciful
and lighter inventions, all given coherence and held together by the
underlying bass line. Taken alone, without the melodic lightness of
flower and leaf, plants that possess the greatest mass—evergreens, hedging plants, and the skeletons of great forest trees—would make somber
music indeed, and, to most gardeners, monotonous music as well. But
that is the garden in winter, when the crucial presence of mass becomes
most important. Few gardeners would substitute the garden in winter,
even granting its austere charm, for a garden full of summer's beauty.
Still, winter is the best time to evaluate the contribution mass makes to
the garden.

Symmetry

So ingrained in human beings is the love of symmetry that it is almost impossible to avoid it. All gardeners know the difficulty, for example, of planting bulbs in natural-seeming drifts; the subconscious desire to place them equidistant from one another in perfectly regular patterns can only be foiled by scattering them randomly on the ground and planting them just where they happen to fall. And could one count the number of doorways where perfectly symmetrical, tight-clipped shrubs stand like sentinels on duty? Our dwellings, too, are overwhelmingly symmetrical in their arrangement, of central door and flanking windows and centered chimney; or if they are not so, they are so self-consciously not so as to affirm powerfully the authority of what they deny.

This pleasure in symmetry must to a great degree originate from the way it reflects our own bodies. We are more or less symmetrical creatures, at least on the outside. And certainly a pleasing symmetry of features is the first part of what makes a human body attractive. But among natural creatures we are not unique in being so fashioned, for most living things—dogs and cats, pigs and jellyfish, daisies and spruce trees—are symmetrically arranged, simply as a result of the regularity with which cells divide.

"Divide" is indeed the key word, for cells grow by one becoming two—and two, or multiples of two, becomes the rule for all symmetry.

But if symmetry is a common attribute of individual living bodies, it occurs in the natural landscape only as a rare and essentially random accident. Nature possesses no sense of order and balance as we know it. The hills are piled up, the valleys carved, and the streams caused to meander through them according to other laws. And the forest grows up with no self-conscious avoidance of regular patterns, for it is random from the first falling of seeds upon the ground, and a thousand accidents control the shape of the mature woods. All these things can, of course, be very beautiful, but they are often given point by human interventions. So those things that often make of the rural landscape a vast and magnificent garden—roads lined with great old maples in regular ranks, the orderly grids of apple orchards, corn growing row on tidy row, a well-placed farmhouse—display always the human love of symmetry and balance.

It must always be remembered about gardens that they reflect man's most intense efforts at arranging nature. Whether in the formal or the natural style, they are, as Pope remarked, "nature methodized." Sometimes the manipulating human will is consciously celebrated. The beautiful order of Filoli in California, or much of Russel Page's work—at Longleat in Wiltshire, England, for example, or at Kiluna on Long Island—force nature without apology into highly patterned and symmetrical arrangements. And for all the richness of planting that great formal gardens can sometimes display, their quiet serenity usually results from a perfect obedience to the values of symmetry and balance. They simply do not permit the assumption that one is in the natural world; rather, one is in a curious hybrid, nature as a reflection of man.

But not all gardens seek so bluntly to celebrate the human control of nature. Sometimes the garden is thought of as another kind of fiction, something seemingly natural, even accidental. But no true garden is an accident, and the most natural-seeming of them is still a tremendously contrived affair. Nor do natural gardens lack symmetry. In them there will almost always be found some frankly symmetrical feature or planting, usually associated with the house or its outbuildings. There will be a terrace of good proportions, a regular level walk leading to the front door, or perhaps a graceful pergola or rectangular arbor for shade or for summer meals. At the least, the door itself will be flanked by a matching pair of boxwoods or lilacs, and where plants for culinary use are grown, in the vegetable and herb garden, the arrangement is almost always symmetrical.

Even those gardens that seem to exclude symmetry altogether will be found to reflect it in a subtler form, which is balance. Like symmetry, balance asks us to see the garden as made up of parts that reflect other parts

along an axis; but whereas symmetry depends on the exact repetition of one part by another, as a mirror image, balance depends on the reflection of part by part, as in the waters of a pond. A rose garden set out on each side of a wide path might thus be bordered on one side by a tall hedge of yew, while on the other, its openness to lawn might be interrupted by a regular sequence of trimmed arborvitaes, not a continuous hedge, but a reflection, in their texture and form, of the solidity of the yew.

In achieving balance, the essential point is that each unit be a response to the principal value of the one that lies opposite, or nearly opposite, to it. So, if the chief attribute of a plant is its texture of leaf, as is the case with rhododendrons, its value might be balanced by a planting of leucothoe or *Ilex* x *meserveae,* since the structural contributions of all these plants are in their thick, dark, evergreen foliage, whatever other pleasures they may offer of seasonal bloom or berry. When form is the principal attribute of a plant, as with a column of dark-green yew, balance might be achieved by the upright form ('Columnaris') of the deciduous *Rhamnus frangula,* often sold under the popular name of "tallhedge." Balance can occur not only in the vertical, however, but also in the horizontal, and so a planting of ground-hugging juniper might be reflected by a low planting of deciduous, red-berried cotoneaster. And occasionally, a wonderfully subtle sense of balance may be achieved by working a horizontal form against a vertical one, as when the upright form of a Hinoki false cypress is as tall as a flat-growing evergreen across the path—*Microbiota decussata,* for example—is wide.

Symmetry will always be more obvious than its kindred value, balance. But the point of both is the same. Both reflect the degree of calculation with which the seasonal and superficial beauties of the garden have been underlaid, achieving a deeper structure than the eye often registers and one more satisfying than the conscious mind acknowledges. For although both symmetry and balance must be consciously created in gardens, they reflect a preference buried below our minds and in our actual physical beings.

Shape

*P*lants make their most forceful contribution to a garden not through their flowers, or even through their foliage, but through their shapes. It is the lines of a plant that create the complex structure of wall and hedge, glade and coppice, bay and plain that is the garden. And as we inhabit the garden not only during the brief months of summer but in spring, fall, and winter, too, we must establish its essential design with plants whose shapes are arresting throughout the year. So, despite their vogue, herbaceous perennials, which for many people are the whole of a garden, are of secondary importance in a garden's making. Woody plants—trees and shrubs, deciduous and evergreen—are its essential components.

All plants have shapes, but not all shapes are equally pleasing. Some plants seem to grow in a kind of random disregard of their own best form, thrusting themselves this way and that, concerned only with filling space and exposing as much leaf surface as possible to the light. Among the familiar plants gardeners cherish, roses are the best example of woody shrubs whose shape, left to itself, is of little value. Although there are some exceptions among species roses, gardeners mostly tolerate a graceless form for the charm of the flowers, and sometimes for the brilliantly colored hips.

Other plants, however, shape themselves in ways so felicitous as to justify their place in gardens by their branches alone, whatever other beauties they offer of leaf, flower, or foliage. I think here of *Fothergilla gardenii*, a lovely shrub native to the American South (but hardy well into zone 4) whose many stems, whimsically crooked, never seem congested. Despite its white, bottlebrush flowers in May, its handsome pleated leaves in summer, and its brilliant scarlet and yellow autumn color, I still prefer it in winter, when the charm of its twigs and branches, all arranged with perfect grace, becomes most apparent.

Lilacs, too, make their most valuable contribution to a garden by their shape. The flowers, in every shade from the richest purple-violet to pink, white, and even ivory-yellow, are rightly treasured; and, of course, there is no smell quite like the smell of lilacs, borne on warm night breezes in that brief and most evocative moment between spring and summer. But their flowering period is short, and their leaves, even when free of mildew, are hardly good enough to justify planting them. It is the shape of their wood, gaunt, stern, and sinuous, mottled with patches of white and crusted with lichens, that really earns them their secure place in gardens.

The range of shapes that plants present is enormous. There are columns, vases, mounds, tufts, and carpets, shapes both densely congested and gracefully attenuated, rigidly vertical and absolutely horizontal. To this plethora of forms attentive gardeners have added refinements, noting and propagating natural mutations and selectively breeding for pronounced growth habits. Doublefile viburnum (*V. plicatum* var. *tomentosum*), already an exciting plant for its shape, exists in two cultivars selected for even more pronounced horizontal branching patterns, 'Lanarth' and 'Mariesii'. The great white spruce of the Northern American forests (*Picea glauca*) occurs in the cultivar 'Conica' as a densely congested cone of fine texture that never needs pruning to keep its formal shape. The spreading English oak (*Quercus robur*) occurs in a tight vertical column in the cultivar 'Fastigiata', and the New England sugar maple (*Acer saccharum*) can be had in two upright forms towering to fifty feet high but only twelve feet wide, the cultivars 'Newton Sentry' and 'Temple's Upright'. And the number of shapes offered by the Canadian hemlock (*Tsuga canadensis*)—arching, weeping, contorted, layered, rounded,

and creeping—could fill a large garden by themselves alone, were the gardener so minded.

But even this rich abundance does not exhaust the plenitude of shapes and forms plants can take. For beyond those they assume naturally are those they can be given through artifice. With secateurs and shears, stakes and twine, the gardener can shape plants into forms both seemingly natural and self-consciously contrived. A remarkable instance of contrived form grew for years in Radcliffe Yard, in Cambridge, Massachusetts. There was there (and may be still) an ancient crab apple, probably *Malus hupehensis,* the main trunk of which snaked along the ground for perhaps twenty feet, producing upright sinewy secondary trunks along its length to form a little forest. Whether the result of some accident the tree experienced in youth, or (more probably) the work of some clever gardener, the result was extraordinary, at once eccentric and venerable.

Of all the formal shapes given to plants—pyramids, neat-lined hedges, lollipops, kettledrums, topiary peacocks, or teapots and other fancies—

none are more beautiful than the shapes given to fruit trees. For centuries, apples, pears, quinces, and other fruits have been trained on forms against walls, or freestanding, in fans, cordons, palms, and the interlocking diamond shape called a Belgian fence. Called espaliers from the trelliswork on which they were originally trained, they evolved from the purely utilitarian concerns of maximizing space and trapping the heat of walls and buildings for early ripening. But they are beautiful as well, so much so that the gardeners at the Luxembourg Gardens, in Paris, have preserved the entire severed trunk and branches of a perfectly espaliered pear tree in their workroom. It was started early in the seventeenth century and has been dead for at least fifty years. Still, it is a textbook of the way to do it, and an object of great beauty.

There is no garden, from the most highly formal and mannered to the simplest and most romantic, that does not owe much of its beauty to the careful manipulation of plant shapes. Often those shapes are very assertive, as when a line of sternly clipped pyramidal yews and low hedges of box give form to beds of tea roses or annuals. Just as often, however, they may seem to have come by accident, as when a dark-green column of juniper rises from a sea of heather, or when slender rods of a red-stemmed dogwood (*Cornus alba* 'Siberica') cluster against the black mass of a pine. But more perhaps than for any other major principle of garden design, it is difficult to give rules for shape. Most often, the eye of the gardener returns again and again to a corner of the garden, a flat plane of growth that needs a vertical emphasis, a loose and airy mass that craves a strong columnar shape, the bare shanks of shrubs that could be knit together by a low ribbonlike drift, or the blank wall of a garage that might be clothed by an espalier, whether a classic one of apple or pear or a looser, more spontaneous one of forsythia or flowering quince. Eventually the eye, nagged and nagged, comes up with the missing shape, and the puzzle is solved.

Happily, also, shape is one of the easiest of design considerations to translate from garden to garden, or even from gorgeous picture books to one's own modest plot. When a picture or a spot in a living garden seems particularly beautiful, one should always pause, for as long as need be, to answer the great garden question, *"What makes this work?"* Often it will not be the beauty of the flowers or the fullness of the leaves or the rarity of the plants, but the fine articulation of one shape against another. And by a quick, crude sketch that isolates those shapes, even people who cannot draw their route out of a country town can bring magic home. For be the plant ever so rare or old or particular in its requirements, it is the shape that counts, and an equivalent shape can always be found.

Repose

It is one of the inevitable and unfortunate correlations of gardening that the more the gardener loves plants, the more difficult it becomes to achieve the quality of repose. The very love of plants that may bring the gardener to attempt a garden in the first place can often rob that garden of the quiet stillness that we recognize as among its chief pleasures. A garden is, after all, conceived of as a haven, a refuge against the press of the world, a place set apart to be ruled by order, beauty, and serenity. But the enthusiasm with which the gardener often pursues his passion too frequently can result in a garden that, although it may be rich, complex, and striking, is anything but quiet.

Stating the issue this way is, of course, to build up a false dichotomy between serene gardens on the one hand and those rich and complex with the endless fascination of plants on the other. Within a good garden, whatever its size, the conflicting impulses of the spiritualist and the materialist can be reconciled, but not without an awareness of the problem and the conscious willingness to work out its resolution. For all gardens worthy of the name are not so much planted as *composed*.

The surest way to a feeling of repose in a garden is first to balance those parts that are complex and highly worked with the parts that are simple and quiet. In many gardens, there can be no better balance than that offered by expanses of mown grass, which create ponds of repose lapping against the shores of borders vivid with flowers or thick with masses of shrubbery. Although shrinking the lawn or eliminating it altogether has become a kind of credential for the serious gardener (even the "moral" gardener), I can think of nothing so conducive to a sense of repose as a generous greensward. Of course, it is not for all climates. But other expansive, neutral surfaces may work as well—raked gravel, for example, or large flat slabs of stone, softened by creeping thymes or other mat-forming plants that love to be dry and baked by the sun, or, in shade, by gentle mosses and small ferns. Whatever the material, the principle is the same: to counter much with little, to offset abundance with restraint.

As important as a flat and quiet plane of grass or gravel or stone in achieving repose is the use of the large gesture. Particularly with herbaceous plants, it is important to create large drifts of seven or twelve or fifteen individuals in a species, enough to make their use seem to be the stroke of nature's hand rather than a niggling, arbitrary human caprice. Such bold plantings run contrary to the gardener's urge to grow all his favorite plants, all together, one of this, one of that, and one of the other. And in very confined gardens, a chafing restraint may be necessary if repose is to be the result. But in gardens of more ample size, a secluded place can usually be found—a bit of rockery, a cutting garden, a corner of the vegetable plot—where the collector's impulse can run free, and where the gardener can go when his energies are high and when the balm of repose is not what he is seeking. From such places he may be glad to retreat, at the end of a day of fiddling and a surfeit of color, to quieter, more restrained parts of the garden, where only a few species, in large groups, rest the eye, the spirit, and even the muscles.

Another device useful in achieving repose is that of repetition. In formal gardens, where hedges, topiaries, and paths form an ordered rhythm, repose is easy to achieve, although its younger sibling, tedium, may quickly shoulder it away. In informal gardens, those preferred by most Americans, the repetition of elements, even of rather formal elements, is no less valuable and far less subject to such sibling rivalry. So the disheveled and untidy tumble of a garden of old roses might be given order by the repetition of columnar evergreens, by fat, rounded cushions of boxwood, or even by the glossy foliage of peonies out of flower. In a perennial garden, exuberant with bloom, one plant of quaint and beautiful leaf, such as silvery *Artemesia ludoviciana,* might be repeated at regular intervals to draw the eye in a quiet rhythm over the whole. And even in the "wild" garden, an ordered sequence of strong, repeated shapes—the pyramids of native hemlocks and junipers or columns of yew—could add, by their solidity of form, a quality of repose to the lush tumble of lesser plants around them. In such situations, the ordered repetition of strong and rather formal shapes may not, indeed should not, be an overly assertive element in the design, calling into compromise the overall

intent of the garden. Rather, the repetition of strong shapes should be somewhat recessive, almost, but not quite, subsumed in the general abundance and seeming spontaneity of the plantings, but contributing, still, a strong, restful rhythm to the whole.

If the garden itself is a quiet retreat from the busy world, one sometimes craves within it a still further retreat, even from the garden itself. No one knows better than the gardener the degree to which its beauty is won by unrelenting and often exhausting labor, a labor that is really never done. Sometimes a place apart, one that asks little and does not confront the roving, anxious eye with the chores of deadheading, raking, pruning, tying in, tying up, cutting back, dividing, replanting . . . is necessary to the gardener's sanity and even to the garden's continued existence. The gardener needs a resting spot, where he can sit and stare, and such spots should be literally hidden away, sheltered all around, out of sight, not only of the world but of the garden itself.

In my own garden this place is a small, round terrace of fieldstone, covered almost over with mosses and surrounded by sturdy "common" shrubs of the easiest care, *Viburnum dentatum, Berberis* x *mentorensis,* and *Enkianthus campanulatus.* Around their ankles are swirls of ground cover, gentle, glossy-leaved myrtle, blue-eyed in spring, and patches of *Geranium macrorrhizum,* pine-scented on a hot summer day and softly pumpkin-colored in autumn. There is hardly a weed to pull, and there is a seat, an old weathered stone nicely flat on top, convenient only for one person and too low to jump up from in a hurry. The labor of prying it out of the neighboring field and setting it just where it rests is all but forgotten. It is there forever. But so am I not, for I confess that I seldom settle in this spot for rest. It exists mostly as a possibility, a feeling in the mind, as repose, in gardens, always does.

Time

Gardens, like the gardeners who make them, grow old. And as the youthful garden has about it all the enthusiasm, exuberance, color, and experimentation that marks the young, so, we hope, old gardens, too, reflect the character of their now less-youthful makers. And in a culture that, while freely acknowledging the virtues and joys of youth, seems to have forgotten that beauty also attends old age, gardens offer testimony to the repose, order, and serenity that age alone can bring.

The surest road to just this beauty rests on one principle: In our gardens, as in our lives, the old must not pretend that they are young. The realities that age imposes must be embraced for what they are, and the virtues that flow from them must be cultivated. In gardens, the first of these realities is the steady increase of shade. As gardeners grow older, their gardens grow shadier. The trees we planted years ago with hope and optimism—the *Acer griseum* for its peeling, cinnamon-red bark, the *Magnolia* x *soulangiana* 'Alba Superba' for its muscular form and its scented white chalices in April, the Washington thorn for its craggy, congested shape and its clusters of scarlet fruit in November—all have thrived, gaining increased presence and beauty with age. But where around them once grew phlox, veronicas, irises, and asters, now there must be hostas, ferns, and gingers, for the shade they cast requires the gentler, quieter companions of the woodland.

The second reality that age imposes on the garden is that there will be fewer plants in it; for the process of aging in a garden is most often a process of editing. Gardens occupy finite spaces. Whatever grows does so at the expense of something else. Where there was once room for three

small trees, several shrubs, and sixty perennials, there may now remain room for only one tree and two drifts of perennials, all grown vastly larger. The restraint imposed on the garden by age may be as hard on the passionate gardener as the restraints imposed by life; but if one is wise, one will recognize that less is, paradoxically, more. For if there are fewer plants in the mature garden, those that remain have a presence, a larger authority, a fullness in themselves that no greater number of youthful plants can possess. One great tree of *Cladrastis kentukea,* with an elephantine trunk and a thousand scented racemes of wisterialike flowers in early summer, may be compensation for the vivid hues of all the perennials that once flourished in the space it has finally come to claim. Few gardeners would have it down just to plant more daylilies.

Of course, most gardeners, like most young people, do not plan for age from the start. There may be wise old youths, and wise young gardeners, who from the beginning of the venture have their twenty-five-year plans in mind and their retirement funds in order. If so, I wish them luck, for the garden, like life, has a curious way of surprising one; and in both, far more is gained by taking advantage of what is offered than by slavishly sticking to the plan. Most gardeners go at the business of making a garden in a merry heedlessness of time; we plant what we like, and with abandon, hoping that it will all come out well in the end.

Left alone, it seldom does. For the more vigorous plants will prevail and the weaker will perish. Even those that survive will do so at some cost, both to themselves and to those around them. They will be disfigured by the struggle for light and space, shaded out on this side or that, bent and twisted—perhaps picturesquely but as likely not—by the fight for life. Much may, of course, be done to regulate this struggle by wielding the pruning shears and saw, and by relocating shrubs and small trees. Careful choices of what one plants go some distance in avoiding the laws of the jungle. Those choices, if one is capable of the wisdom required, should be made quite early in the life of the garden. Plants have an uncanny way of winning our affections, however, and never more so than in infancy and thriving youth. But the spruce or pine that charms us in its five-gallon nursery can, that seems the perfect vertical accent for the new rose border, will be bent on achieving the sixty feet of height that is

its inborn destiny, hack at it although we may. Better by far to pass it over for an Alberta spruce that will assume its majority at six feet, or even a yew, initially perhaps a boring choice but one that will accept a periodic shave and that can be relocated easily should the roses grow far fuller than we ever hoped they could.

Imagining the garden as it will someday be is, however, for most of us, an impossible discipline. We see what is there, not what will be, and few of us are prepared to plant only for effects thirty or forty years in the future. We plant for this summer or next, or, if we are very forward-thinking, for five or even ten years hence. And, of course, we plant on impulse, because in a visit to the garden center or on our travels, we give way to the charms of this or that plant, hoping that somehow we can find the space for it to grow. That is simply the way gardeners are made, pretend to fight it though we may. It is a poor gardener—and probably a poor garden—where this is not so.

Fortunately, however, greater strength of will comes with age, when the challenges are so much greater. However much forethought and restraint have attended the making of the young garden, if the old garden is to assume the spare and dignified beauty of which it is capable, the gardener who controls it must be prepared to give things up. He must not add but subtract, often destroying just those plants he has nurtured. But what the gardener must nurture above everything else is not one plant or another, but the garden itself for as long as he is its steward. It is in the choice of what remains that the beauty of the mature garden, and the art that makes it, inhere.

Part II

Practice

Foundation Plantings

Foundation plantings, that is, the shrubbery arranged along a house front to conceal its often unattractive underpinnings, are perhaps the most cliché-ridden element in American horticulture. Even when the house is home to a serious gardener, the plantings clustered about the main entrance are too often simply variants on a ubiquitous national formula. That formula—a pair of evergreens at the door, some taller shrubs at the corners and lower shrubs mixed up in between—is repeated dooryard by dooryard all across the land without regard to climate, terrain, horticultural possibilities, or even the architecture of the house itself. Frequently, the undistinguished inhabitants of such foundation plantings are allowed to grow beyond all reclaiming, producing an effect of gloom and oppression; worse, the national passion for wielding the hedge clippers creates a mad rhythm of ugly shapes—pyramids and boxes and kettledrums all in a row. The result is bad, boring plantings across the fronts of millions of American homes, houses that are in themselves attractive and could be made beautiful by more sensitive treatments.

Anyone concerned with the beauty of growing things will have some difficulty in understanding the intent behind such plantings. Perhaps they are a consequence of our political mythology, which expects us to present an egalitarian sameness to the world. More probably, however, they result from the need imposed on builders to clean up the mess they have made of the landscape and domesticate the rawness of their work. A commonly acknowledged forumla that satisfies the decencies and doesn't cost much is to their liking, and the clipped hemlock, yew, arborvitae, and potentilla they leave behind tend to stay. All these plants are good ones, the bread and butter of wholesale nurserymen for their ease of propagation, their relative freedom from pests and diseases, their capacity to transplant readily, and their ability to make a decent show—initially—in poor and unimproved soil. All have their uses in the landscape; but whether the best one is to be clustered along raw cement foundations in a disharmonious mishmash of forms, any drive through a new suburb must call into doubt.

To think freshly about foundation plantings, we need first to ask what function they serve. There are, of course, many houses that sit up in the air on high, exposed, and often ugly foundations. Here the massing of shrubbery along the front may be necessary to mask the offending foundation and anchor the house to the ground. But even in such cases, a genuine fondness for plants can suggest other, more original solutions than the ones we are used to seeing. I know a house with just this problem that is—happily for the rest of us—inhabited by a passionate lover of alpines, the tiny mats and tuffets that grow on high mountains above the tree line. Faced by the necessity of masking almost four feet of ugly cement, the gardener built a stone wall before it, filling the space between with gravelly earth, in which she planted treasures, both between the stones as she built and over the top of the bed. The result was a miniature world of small plants, fascinating in foliage and flower and changing with the seasons, most charming perhaps when viewed from within the house. The insulating properties of such a design were not her main concern, though they were, of course, an advantage.

Not all high foundations are built of materials that can support a raised stone bed, and not all exposures and architectural styles are appropriate to such treatment. It is true, also, that one of the challenges of creating interesting foundation plantings is to bring them into harmony with those that neighbor them, up and down the street. For no garden effect should seem anomalous and startling, especially one facing the public view. A subtle difference, a finer eye, a more interesting choice of plants will all be gain, but only if the results blend with what lies around. Although generally one may do whatever one pleases to the back and sides of a house, expressing any garden fantasy or horticultural interest one might possess, along the street one may be limited to some degree by

convention. That is not to say that one's plantings need be banal and completely predictable.

One specific example might be offered to illustrate this point. Everywhere in America, in cities and in suburbs, are high Victorian houses with elevated porches and six-foot-tall exposed underpinnings, often of wood or brick pilings sheathed in lattice. The shallow plots that often exist between the house and sidewalk are usually filled with nondescript overgrown shrubs, yew, hydrangea, bush honeysuckle, forsythia, privet, or whatever else was cheap, sturdy, and capable of bulking large. I know of one such house that received a more effective approach. The high foundation along the porch was wrapped in a narrow, severely trimmed hedge of fastigiate yew, the tailored outline of which served to create a quiet, unifying foil for the rich architectural detail of the house. The scrap of ground between the house and sidewalk, disencumbered of pointless volumes of leaf and twig, was planted with a quiet ground cover of *Sasa pygmea*, a rampant, dwarf bamboo that really could only be released in an area contained by the house, its own and the neighbor's drive, and the sidewalk. One large flowering shrub, a multistemmed witch hazel, was placed strategically and slightly off-center in the square of ground and was allowed to grow in a natural shape to the stature almost of a small tree. The result, though simple, was attractive at all seasons—in winter, when the dark backdrop of yew gave contrast to the silver-gray of the witch hazel stems, in early spring, when the witch hazel burst into thousands of rust-red thrums of highly fragrant flowers, and in summer, when the fresh foliage of the bamboo created a cool, almost tropical, effect. This planting, beautiful in itself, is also suggestive of other possibilities; for although the yew was probably obligatory, and not to be bettered for what it did, the bamboo might have been replaced with *Vinca minor*, perhaps the white-flowered form for special interest, or with Epimedium. An alternative to the witch hazel might have been a multistemmed specimen of *Magnolia stellata*, or, where space was very limited, a single, tall, deciduous white azalea.

Perhaps the most challenging of all foundation planting problems occurs when a ranch house, with exposed foundations, possesses overhanging eaves that make the establishment of plants difficult. Such houses are designed to provide welcome shade within, and typically occur in the Deep South or Far West, where summer heat is oppressive. The problem they create is one of the most difficult for the gardener— that of dry shade. Even with constant and perhaps costly irrigation, the range of plants that will flourish in such conditions is limited and often boring. A far better solution than planting out the foundations of such houses might be to mulch the space beneath the eaves with gravel or small stones and face the offending concrete with stucco or perhaps veneer it with brick, clapboard, or siding to match or complement the siding of the house itself. Imaginative plantings of flowering shrubs or ornamental grasses can then be grouped beyond the eaves, and where there is space, the gravel or stone can provide a walkway to other por- tions of the garden, as is often the case with houses in Japan. Such a path might even be shaded by a pergola or arbor connected to the eaves, pro- viding additional shade within and a leafy retreat from the broiling sun.

Though national prejudice argues strongly against it, not every house actually needs a foundation planting. Many houses are set close to the ground or possess foundations of stone or brick that are attractive in themselves and do not require disguise. The lines of such houses are suf- ficiently pleasing that they can be left alone, to sit simply on the earth. A wide skirt of ground cover might be enough, with a vine or small flower- ing or fruiting tree espaliered against the wall to tie the house to the ground. The shrubbery that would have been arrayed against the house in a traditional foundation planting can instead be set at the outer bor- ders of the yard, creating a frame that demarcates the property from the world beyond, making even of the front yard a haven of quiet free from the public gaze.

Often, when the existing foundation plantings of such a property are redesigned, even quite large shrubs can be relocated to provide a part of this frame. Most plants used in foundation plantings (particularly yews, pieris, and rhododendrons) can be moved at almost any age, given the muscle and the will to do it. Occasionally, a single large specimen by a door or at the corner of the house can be left in place, or shifted, to attain new dignity when freed from its crowding companions and to provide an anchor for a rich herbaceous border full of early bulbs and, later, of summer-flowering perennials. For although herbaceous plants seldom look good as the principal components of a foundation planting, the creation of a frame of shrubbery at the perimeter of the property can result in a true cottage garden, where tall delphiniums, peonies, daylilies, foxgloves, and a host of other wonderful border plants replace the yews and junipers once grouped there. Better still, there might be two borders, one against the house and another against the outer wall of shrubs, with a wide grass path between, thus creating a pleasing balance.

It is the essence of the traditional foundation planting that it presents an unchanging face to the world in summer, fall, winter, and spring. But the true gardener loves the progress of the seasons, and joys in observing them, below the windows of the house in the morning with coffee in hand and turning into the drive at twilight after a hard day of work. Once freed from the tyranny of the traditional foundation planting, the front of the house, most prominent both to the gardener and to passersby, can magically reflect the changing year. My own house, a simple, weathered farmhouse of gray clapboard, is planted with five large, native deciduous hollies, *Ilex verticillata*. In fifteen years they have reached the eaves of its roof, and spread a loose curtain of green before its windows in summer, providing cooling shade within. But in late autumn, when the leaves drop, each branch is laden with sparkling red berries, sprays of scarlet against the gray of the house. Sometimes, flocks of purple grossbeaks light on the branches to feed on the fruit, not two feet from where I sit and watch them. And in early spring, just after the snows have melted, thick colonies of *Scylla siberica* spread a carpet of cerulean blue beneath their gaunt trunks. I do not much miss the yews and junipers that might have been there.

Lawns and Ground Covers

I have a friend, a committed New Yorker, who has recently fulfilled her lifelong dream of acquiring a place in the country. It has been, by and large, a successful venture. She has taken with enthusiasm to the rituals of country life, and the vegetable garden, the compost pile, and the woodlot have all richly repaid the efforts they require. Zucchini in wagon loads return to the city with her each Sunday, and the delivery to her office of shiny new tools, fresh with green paint and unblemished ash wood handles lightens the end of the workweek and adds zest to antici-pated weekends. But one essential component of ex-urban life aggravates her out of all humor. She calls it her "yawn," and that is all it provokes in her beyond the enormous annoyance at the tyranny it exercises over her precious Saturdays and Sundays.

I myself am very fond of lawns and can't imagine being without at least a scrap of one. But I see that my friend has too much, and, in that, she is like most people. Gardens in America often consist of little else, with per-haps a tree or two set in for shade and a narrow bed for flowers along the edge. To tend them well requires prodigious expenditures of time and money. They must be fed, weeded, watered, thatched, and, of course, mowed and raked with relentless regularity. Even with all this effort, most lawns in North America fulfill the scathing description of one visiting Englishman, that they are "but elevated pasture." Like so many garden effects we inherit and perpetuate, they should be rethought.

One must begin by acknowledging that lawns, wide sweeps of grass, emerald-green, freshly cut to perfect smoothness, rolling gently from property to property along spacious tree-lined suburban streets, have a powerful hold on the American imagination. It was on them that we first learned to walk, to play ball, to improve our high school tans, to savor summer barbecues of fresh corn and charcoal-grilled hamburgers, perhaps to flirt with the girl or boy next door. They are part of our national myth, and it is not a bad thing for any nation to cling to its myths, even if, under the press of the growing complexity of modern life, our increased awareness of ecological facts and the steady decrease in the

time we had once to do what we remember as very pleasant, we must reduce our myths a bit, mow them down, as it were, to size.

Essentially, lawns serve both a practical and an aesthetic function. Practically, they are outdoor rooms, and in the fine months of summer they are probably more used than the living room, dining room, or kitchen, for they may pleasantly perform the functions of all three. Aesthetically, their quiet, uniform surface and their restful color provide a foil against which other elements in the garden—shade trees, shrubs, perennial borders—gain added value, as does the house itself. They are carpet, upon or against which other things are set.

The metaphor of the room, always stimulating when thinking of gardens, is never more so than in the consideration of lawns. For if lawns are the carpet of outdoor rooms, those rooms must have walls. Although the ideal, one might say the mythical, American lawn is one that rolls down to the street and seamlessly from property to property, it is an ideal born of a time when American life was perhaps more homogenized, but certainly when American streets were quieter, traversed only by the iceman, the newspaper boy on his bicycle, and an occasional car.

Privacy and quiet have become national appetites, as has the desire for more time to do what we wish rather than what we must. So the reduction of lawns to accommodate walls of shrubbery, with borders of flowers against them, gives us privacy to enjoy our outdoor rooms and frees up at least some of the time once devoted to mowing, raking, feeding, and watering—time that may now be spent on more rewarding garden activities. And the lawn, bordered by defining walls and reduced in extent, is itself more beautiful, gaining new value as a horizontal foil against a vertical one, catching the play of light and shadow from small trees and taller shrubs grouped around its verges. That there is less of it means also that it may be better tended, which is in itself a gain.

Lawns may be reduced in extent and heightened in value in ways other than by defining walls of shrubbery against which shade or sunloving perennials may be grouped. Or perhaps it would be better to say "in additional ways," for the value of a frame in a garden, for definition and for privacy, should never be forgotten. But wide beds of ground cover may also be introduced, before the house in ample beds, or perhaps as a low-maintenance foil to trees and shrubs massed at the property's edge. Serviceable *Vinca minor* and ubiquitous *Pachysandra terminalis* can, in eastern gardens, still achieve a quiet, dignified beauty if they are planted generously, are well edged, and are kept in emerald-green health. Where it grows well, *Hedera helix,* English ivy in many forms, some mottled, variegated, or cut-leaved, can also be rich and wonderful. Indeed, anything low and dense enough of growth to smother weeds, and reasonably self-maintaining once established, can be massed against a lawn to reduce its extent and add an additional horizontal plane to the garden. It is true, of course, that most plants usually considered to be ground covers, and certainly the ones mentioned here, are not among those that give gardeners their greatest thrills of excitement. But that is the point, for in carpeting large surfaces in the garden, a certain attractive blandness is desirable, relieved by an occasional splendid shrub or small tree, but otherwise clothing the ground in seemly and unassertive fashion, as does lawn grass.

It must also be remembered that, although ground cover performs almost all the functions of a lawn, it may not be walked upon. Half the magic of any garden is in walking through it, and so beds of ground cover should be traversed by wide, paved paths that allow us to get from here to there and give us a sense that the garden is meant not merely to be viewed but to be moved through.

More ample sweeps of paving, in the form of terraces or courtyards, are in themselves an exciting alternative to lawns, particularly in those areas of our country where lawn grass does not thrive, or where it thrives at the expense of almost constant watering and feeding. Paving performs the functions we expect of a lawn; practically, it allows easy movement across it and provides space for many outdoor activities; aesthetically, it ties the house to its surroundings and offers a bland horizontal surface against which the vertical elements of the garden gain value. Further, it draws the life of the house outdoors, better than does a lawn, for even after a rain or heavy dew it may be walked on with comfort. There are, indeed, many beautiful gardens in California and the Southwest, in Mexico and in Mediterranean countries, where paved surfaces, with magical effect, have entirely replaced grass. But their magic inheres in an abundant verdure of trees, shrubs, and perennials that press against and soften the pavement, or even seed themselves into its cracks, creating the sense that the stones and plants are one harmonious entity. Even more than with lawns, the paved garden seems to require a frame, of shrubs or masonry or stucco walls, so that it seems a world apart, an oasis.

Still, there will always be American gardeners, and I am one, who will insist on their bit of lawn, who will grudgingly or patiently give it all it craves, who will water, fertilize, mow, seed, and reseed, simply to feel its spring beneath their feet, to rest their eyes on its quiet greenness, to judge the arrival of the first frost by its sugared blackness, the spring by its slow greening and the first robin, extracting from it a worm, and to watch the endlessly fascinating play of light and shadow across its surface. For such addicts of lawn, the question is not whether or not to have one, but rather, how much of one constitutes a precious enough.

Porches, Decks, and Terraces

It is not often that I disagree with Jane Austen. But in her great novel *Emma* (1816) there is an opinion with which I take issue. A party is being planned at the home of the book's hero, Mr. Knightley. A Mrs. Elton, who represents in the novel all that is pretentious and vulgar, expands on how it is to unfold:

> "It is to be . . . a sort of gipsy party. We are to walk about your gardens, and gather the strawberries ourselves, and sit under the trees. . . . It is to be all out of doors—a table spread in the shade, you know. Everything as natural and simple as possible. Is that not your idea?"
>
> "Not quite. My idea of the simple and natural will be to have the table spread in the dining-room."

Although Austen means for us to agree with Mr. Knightley, most Americans, in this debate at least, would tend to side with Mrs. Elton. We appear always to have been an outdoor people, and it would be tempting to consider whether the chuck wagon and the campfire, essential to our

80

experience as colonials in the wilderness, have not left a permanent trace on our national identity. However it comes to be, the picnic and the barbecue are American institutions. Whenever we can, we make a little festival of being out of doors, and certainly of dining there. We may, however, meet the fictional Mr. Knightley at least halfway in his convictions, for we do not generally haul Grandmother's Duncan Phyffe or Hepplewhite out under the trees, assuming she left that to us. Rather, we contrive porches, decks, and terraces where living outdoors can be sensible, bother-free, and comfortable. These structures, essential transitions from house to garden, are one of the few garden improvements on which bank officers will smile. Quite rightly, for they are also valuable components to the enjoyment of the garden and the enjoyment of life.

Of the three features—porches, decks, and terraces—the first is apt to be the one that most frequently comes with the house, although many a plain-Jane house can be transformed into a gracious and architecturally interesting structure by the addition of a porch. Porches can be wonderful things, particularly in warm and sunny climates where their shade and their openness to any passing breeze make them welcome additions to a house. But they may be equally valuable in wet climates, for there they provide a chance to be outdoors when the weather is showery, a place to enjoy the music of the rain or simply to hang out the wash (as is done here in Vermont by people who feel they have little to hide). But porches can also be dank, neglected, cobwebby places, looming above the garden and presenting a barrier to our natural impulse to be out and in it. That is simply to say that, like any other house or garden effect, porches are not guaranteed to be pleasant simply because they are porches. They require careful planning.

More than terraces and decks, a porch is an architectural consideration requiring the skill of a good architect or a local craftsman whose work is proven to evaluate its appropriateness to the house itself and the porch's structural soundness. But the services of a good landscape designer might also be secured in order to determine how an existing porch or one proposed as an addition can best be an enhancement to the garden. For a porch, when spacious, well built, well furnished, and successfully related to the landscape around it, offers to a greater degree than any other garden structure the magical sense of being both indoors and outdoors at once. Furniture too fragile for exposure to the elements can be left there, in attractive groupings complete with bright cloth cushions and pots of shade-loving flowers and cool ferns. A flowering vine, perhaps a wisteria or a honeysuckle, can be trained about the eaves, forming a green curtain and a fragrant bower of shade. Tall evergreens or old-fashioned flowering shrubs might be grouped below it, their tops just equal to its floor. There should be a swing, certainly, and as often as possible a frosty pitcher of lemonade or of iced tea. It is clear that such a picture tugs at our collective national memory, and those over whom it has most power will want nothing else.

Decks might well be considered a sort of midway structure between porches and terraces. Like porches, decks are made of wood, and when attached to a wooden house, provide both a structural and a material transition from house to garden; like terraces, however, decks are open to the elements, suggesting much of the expansiveness we often associate with lawns. But the emotional resonances of decks are quite different from either those of porches or of terraces. The word is nautical and suggests an adventurous, free-floating quality. Decks are, in fact, best when they convey this feeling of being on a raft perhaps, with the plants of the garden pressing close about; or of being in a tree house, surveying the terrain (but not, if it can be helped, the neighbors) from a platform high above the surrounding vegetation. Two specific problem areas in gardens are often best solved—and turned into assets—by the construction of a deck. The first is low, poorly drained ground, where a deck just above ground level can float amid rich, almost tropical-seeming plants that love a damp spot, plants such as *Petasites japonicus* var. *giganteus* and *Darmera peltata,* and semiacquatic irises and grasses such as *Iris pseudacorus* and *Miscanthus floridulus.* The second is a steeply sloping site to the back or side of a house, where a deck will extend outdoor living space scarcely otherwise usable, and will allow one to sit among the tops of the forest trees and peer down at a rich understory of shade-loving smaller trees and shrubs, dogwoods, witch hazels, rhododendrons, and the like.

Wooden decks are enormously popular throughout the country, for they are the least expensive way of achieving a hard-surfaced outdoor living area, and their construction is not beyond the local handyman or even the unskilled house owner. But decks are not appropriate to all areas or all house styles. They are best where the climate is warm and dry, or where stiff breezes periodically blow away muggy conditions. In dank, wet climates, they can become slimy with algae; and although that algae might eventually support moss, creating a moody, Japanese sort of effect, it will be treacherous and uncomfortable underfoot. And in climates that know snow and sleety rain, such decks can also become genuinely life-threatening, shovel, sweep, and sand how one will. Decks are also fairly recent concepts, virtually unkown in American garden design before the 1950s, and so they seem best when associated with contemporary house design. Although they can sometimes be tactfully associated with houses of traditional architecture, they can too often also look stuck on to such houses, a concession to economy where more traditional porches and terraces would have better served, at least from an aesthetic point of view.

Then there's the question of the wood itself. If your deck is to be frequently and laboriously painted, you can use almost any wood you please and the effect will be as glossy and spiffy as any millionaire's yacht. Generally, however, most people who want decks want a softer, more natural, and more weathered effect than frequent painting, even in the subtlest shades, can offer. So rot-resistant wood must be used. Both West Coast redwood and East Coast cedar are highly resistant to decay, and both weather to attractive shades that harmonize well with plants. Much less costly—and much less nice—is pressure-treated Southern pine. Apart from any concern you might have for the health of the carpenter who must work with this chemical-laden wood, there are several other reasons why this might be a poor choice for decking. Pressure-treated wood holds its unattractive yellow-green color a long time, looking poisonous whether it is, in fact, or not. And timbers of pressure-treated wood can often be unstable, since they are impregnated with preservatives while still green and stay green, it appears, even after considerable exposure to the elements. So they may twist, crack, or checker in the alternating wet and dry conditions of an outdoor environment.

Of the three outdoor living spaces under consideration, terraces of stone or brick are by far the most elegant and the easiest to integrate attractively into the garden. Nothing consorts so beautifully with plants as stone or brick, for they are of the earth itself, and they may be set on the earth in such a way as to become a part of the garden. Plants can even be allowed to seed themselves in the cracks between stone or brick laid on sand, thus intensifying the harmonious interblending of hard surface and living garden. Further, there is no style of architecture that will not gracefully accommodate a carefully sited terrace of the appropriate materials.

Where stone is used, the first choice is always of stone native to the place, if it is flat, for then the terrace will be of a piece with the boulders and outcroppings in the garden itself or in the surrounding countryside. Where native stone of adequate quality is unavailable, then imported stone can be used, assuming one's pocket is deep enough, for it is always very costly. Imported stone should always be selected with great care, however, for it can often look anomalous when put into place, or its color might be unflattering to the plants around it. Before incurring its expense, the home owner should try to see a garden in which it has been used, never settling for the mounted samples offered by many stone yards. And even if one intends to do the work of laying the terrace oneself, it is wise to talk with an experienced mason, paying for an hour or two of his time, to determine how the stone should best be laid—whether on sand or concrete—what provisions should be made for drainage and heaving from frost, and, especially, what percentage of waste there will be in one's choice of stone, for it will usually come in pallets that may include many fragments too small or too uneven for use in terracing.

For terraces, brick is a very desirable alternative to stone, although it creates a more formal and dressy surface, and so should be in harmony with the house it is meant to enhance. When choosing brick, by far the most important consideration is to be sure that it will withstand the rigors of one's climate; in the East particularly, the most beautiful brick—antique "common" brick salvaged from old warehouses and factories—will quickly become punky and flake away when exposed to repeated freezing and thawing. As an alternative, one may be offered brick suitable for outdoor paving (usually called "water-struck brick"), which, although durable, will sometimes look hard, cold, and somehow institutional, an appearance that no amount of wear or age will soften. Attractive brick that combines the softness of antique weathered brick and the durability of water-struck brick is available, and is worth both the search and the price. But again, before committing to any brick, the home owner should see terraces or walks where it has been used, preferably after they have endured two or three winters. Probably, however, no brick is completely indestructible in harsh climates, and so brick terraces are best laid in sand so that the occasional rotten brick can easily be lifted and replaced.

Although porches are always attached to the house, the siting of terraces and decks depends on the use they are intended to serve. Most will be places to gather socially, to eat and drink, talk or sunbathe, and so they should be attached to the house or be conveniently near it. The closer to the kitchen they are, the better. They should also offer possibilities for sitting in sun or in shade for most of the day and in most seasons. So, if the shadow of the house does not offer some shade, a pergola, arbor, or small tree might be placed to one side. Above all, any outdoor living space should possess privacy and gentle enclosure, so a hedge, trellis, or thick planting of shrubs becomes an important component of these spaces if the whole garden is not enclosed, as much for the feeling of security they give as actually to baffle the gaze of passersby.

Although most people will be concerned chiefly with outdoor living spaces that serve social functions, there are other values, essentially contemplative ones, that such spaces might have. When no one else is around, almost any of the features discussed can provide a spot for the busy gardener to sit, to settle into the garden and stare at it. But the values of contemplation are so important, so spiritually necessary, that a quiet spot might well be contrived just to provide them. Thus, any garden, however small, might include a small terrace tucked into a quiet corner of the shrubbery. Such a place might be thought of as the gardener's study, a place to retire to, sheltered from the world, even from friends, family, and responsibility. It should be a place to read, or to put down the book and think, to come to harmony with oneself and the world beyond. Such a place needn't be large. Indeed, it shouldn't be.

Other Garden Structures

Most gardeners know that the least useful thing to do with a garage is to park the family car in it. Bales of peat moss, bags of fertilizer, rolls of burlap, the fancy chipper that was the big present last Christmas, all are more in need of protection from rain and snow than a mere vehicle. And as the garden grows in scope and the gardener in sophistication, space is required for other needs, as a place to store clay pots, a bench on which to sow seeds and strike cuttings, drawers in which to keep plant labels, catalogs, twine, and all the other essential paraphernalia required by gardening. Soon, perhaps, the garage seems a bit crowded and cluttered—even without the car in it—and the gardener begins to long for a proper potting shed, well lit (which garages seldom are), with shelves for reference books, a rack for tools, bins for sand and perlite and potting compost, and a hope that, with proper facilities, one could at least begin to master the exacting art of tidiness.

Simultaneous with this process, or perhaps coming a little before, is the need to expand domestic space. The family grows, as families will, or the family bank account does, and an addition to the house seems necessary. One begins to think that life really would be nicer with the addition of a proper dining room, a library or office, a guest bedroom perhaps, a larger kitchen or a spacious utility room. Maybe the acquisition of a second car, or a third where there are teenaged children, suggests that a garage in which cars could really be parked is a good idea (for one car can be left in the drive, but not two or three). So one begins to think of building a secondary structure on the property, one that would satisfy some long-felt need, or maybe simply some deep desire to make the family nest a little more capacious, a little more comfortable and handsome.

Whatever purpose a new building is to serve, attention to two principles will help to make it an asset to the garden rather than a liability. First, the new structure should echo the general architectural qualities of the house itself and be made of similar materials. Gardens are by their nature fairly busy and complicated aesthetic entities. They gain in beauty if the buildings that inhabit them have a common character and surface. Second, if a new building is to be freestanding, and is to serve something other than a purely domestic function, it should if possible be set along the length of the garden's boundary and not projected out from it. In this way, the new structure will serve not only the practical purpose for which it was built, but will also become a part of the garden's frame.

On country properties where ownership of the land extends beyond the area given to gardening, the placement of buildings in this way usually poses no problem. Many residential communities, however, have setback provisions that require some footage between the property line and any new construction. Even in these cases an outbuilding can help define the frame of the garden, and the space behind put to valuable use. It may serve purely utilitarian purposes best kept out of sight, such as a composting area or a place to stand a wheelbarrow or garden cart. If by luck the space is sunny, it may serve as a nursery for small treasures, a space for cold frames, a child's garden, or even a place to grow a few tomatoes and some salad crops.

Not all new construction can—or should—be of buildings set apart from the main house. Sometimes the house itself must be added to, extended to accommodate needs integral to the life of the family that inhabits it. Here, too, the practical need for more space can also enhance the aesthetic purposes of the garden, making it also a more pleasant place to be in. Nothing is more valuable in a garden than a protected nook, an enclosed room or courtyard, such as is formed when the addition to a house turns a right angle to it. In cold northern climates, such ells can provide shelter from prevailing winds while catching all the warmth of the sun. In climates where sun and heat are more to be avoided than courted, they can be located to provide cooling shade, sheltered perhaps by a vine and with the reassuring presence of water, still or trickling. Terraces for outdoor sitting are always pleasant when located within such spaces, but even so, their horticultural advantages should not be neglected. Vines and espaliers of tender plants can cover the walls, small creeping plants established in the cracks of the pavers, and pots of annuals stood about for summer bloom. Whatever the climate, plants that might fail in less protected parts of the garden may flourish in the shelter provided by such spaces. Best of all, such areas easily assume a special identity, as distinct garden rooms with a character different from other parts of the garden; such an effect is always to be treasured, and should be intensified, perhaps by a high hedge or by trelliswork where only two building walls exist.

If buildings, whether freestanding or attached, can almost always be placed to provide an asset to the garden, other garden structures—pergolas, arbors, arches, and gazebos—can be more problematic. Of these structures, pergolas and arbors can come off best, for they have a clear function. They exist to support plants, whether grapes or roses, clematis, honeysuckle, or actinidias. They usually also mark a passage from one part of the garden to another, the pergola a kind of hallway between separate rooms, the arbor a doorway. Always they are best when they do that, for the most wonderful gardens are a series of rooms, each with its own special character, resonance, or use. Pergolas built more to a square than a linear configuration can be more a room in themselves, a lovely place for midday outdoor dining or a cool place to rest while watching the shifting patterns of light and shade on the pavement.

I have such a pergola in my own garden, built over the stream that bisects it. It is a sort of covered bridge without a roof, constructed of heavy, pegged, post-and-beam timbers, with a wide-planked floor ample enough to accommodate four benches, two on each side, so that one can look up or down the gorge the stream has carved. Its eventual destiny is to be a support for grapes; the four vines planted at its corners have already made their progress to the top of the uprights, and now will be trained over the top to form a living roof. In summer, one will be able to sit there, cooled by the stream beneath and sheltered from the sun, which, when it falls through grape leaves, acquires a golden softness. Thick clusters of grapes (it is to be hoped) will hang down within, amethysts against green gold. And in winter, the gnarled, severely pruned trunks and stems of the vines will loop across and over the structure, causing it to look (an effect always magical in gardens) half made by man, half by nature.

Happy effects with arbors and pergolas can never come, however, without a certain amplitude and substance. They must never seem cramped, flimsy, or trivial. The frail structures one sees in catalogs, purporting to be honest carpenters' work but really mass-produced and stapled together, never work. Plopped at the entrance to a vegetable or cutting garden or placed over a garden seat, they seem insubstantial, afterthoughts if thoughts at all. Any permanent vine worth growing would swamp them in two years and rot them away in five. Their fragility reminds us painfully of how transitory gardens are, although that ought never to be emphasized, truth though it be. For we know that any garden that is really beautiful must seem as if it has always been and must always be, just as it is. For that reason, if for no other, pergolas and arbors ought to be constructed of the sturdiest materials, rather "overbuilt" as carpenters say, to suggest a long, long life in the garden. And they might as well be constructed on the spot, by a good craftsman, rather than bought through mail order or out of a lot. For everything in a garden ought to seem unique to it, made there just because the spot demanded it.

Worse than catalog-bought arbors are gazebos, which seem most popular in America where no garden exists at all. They are perhaps the most conspicuous example of our national belief that gardens are things one buys through the mail, or perhaps from roadside display yards between used-car lots and fast-food restaurants. Produced in mass, they seldom relate to the particular architecture of a house. They offer room for only two or three people to sit at a time, somewhat uncomfortably, and so are useless for entertaining. Generally set up in the air by steps, they cut one off from the life of the garden rather than allowing one to be in it. And

although they may offer some shade, they generally expose one to wind and to bugs. Worst of all, they are usually built of arsenic-impregnated wood or of redwood, either of which, in addition to suggesting the wrong kind of permanence, must make gardeners concerned with the ecology and their own personal health a little ill at ease. Even in their best examples (which are quite costly) they seem far from the essence of a garden, the essence being that it is built from honest toil, sweaty hands, and a deep sense of particularity, of what might fit in there, just there, and no place else. One can, of course, relieve them from their all too prominent place in the middle of a bad lawn by tucking them, for blessed concealment, at the edges of the garden among embowering shrubbery. That is the thing to do, but it still makes the best of a bad deal.

For the money one might spend on a mass-produced gazebo, one might consider a real summerhouse. They were important features of eighteenth-century gardens, and a few sublime examples still exist. Always they were placed apart from the garden itself, down a shady ramble of shrubs or on the garden's woody edge. The essential value they possessed was that they were somewhat secret from the life of the place, providing a retreat, a place to read, to ponder one's own thoughts and be at peace. Although made of stone in the shape of Doric temples, or fashioned of "rustic" logs and twig work, they suggest, in modern adaptation, a wonderful garden feature.

I have been nagged for years, for example, by the idea of creating such a structure, although not modeled on any eighteenth-century example I remember having seen. My summerhouse would be square, or barely rectangular, for hexagons and octagons often have dreadfully uncompromising angles, both within and without. It would have to be ample enough for eight people to sit comfortably, either on benches along its sides or at a table in the middle for a cold midday lunch. It would be built of sturdy timbers, pegged rather than nailed together, open to the sky or perhaps with an even-span roof, I am not quite sure which. Arches on all four sides would allow for views, although the walls of the building would be sheathed in carpenter-made lattice, and the roof, too, if there were a roof. Boston ivy would be trained against this lattice, for the way in which its fingered leaves provide living shingles. But the whole structure would be painted park-bench green, to fit into its surrounding verdure and to provide a somber foil to the brilliant scarlet and yellow of the ivy's autumn color. The floor of my summerhouse might be of old bluestone, if I could get it, although I might be just as happy with pale, honey-colored pea stone, the crunch of which underfoot would be so delightful. Although I am able to imagine this structure in a rather formal garden of box hedges and perennial borders, I think I would like it better if it were somewhat lost in a scrappy landscape of second-growth oak and juniper, improved perhaps by a generous planting of white rugosa roses for their scent, their autumn color, and their fine tomato-red hips. So lost, it would be a fine place to ramble toward, away from the garden and its cares. The one thing I would not wish my summerhouse to have would be a grand view of the distant hills or the sea or even of the whole of my garden. A tantalizing glimpse of any of these might be admissible. But the point of such a place would surely be that it would be a place apart, complete in itself.

All gardeners dream in this way. That is a great difference between them and mere landscapers. For whereas landscapers see gardens as a necessary dressing around buildings, a sort of seemly clothing, gardeners will think of buildings—especially new ones put up on their very own plot—in terms of how they will enhance the garden. Of course, gardeners will be practical, and they may be deeply concerned about creating structures that will serve the needs of their families, and whatever part of their own needs might be left over when they have finished gardening. But when they anticipate the construction of a new building, even from the first they will wonder what it will do to the garden, and what further gardening it might make possible. Located in just that way, the building will catch the sun, and maybe—just maybe—figs might ripen against its wall. Build the pergola there, and through a dark tunnel one will see the vegetable garden, shining in a plenitude of light. The sunny window of the new kitchen will be perfect for starting seedlings of artichoke, and the cement floor of the new garage . . . Oh, dear . . . how convenient for mixing potting soil! But as buildings are apt to be the most assertive elements within a garden, they must always work in harmony with it, both in their materials and in the spatial relationships they define. In the garden, as in all other arts, the parts must seem inevitable, eminently practical . . . and inspired.

Gardening on Slopes

As in other ways, gardening reflects high art in that the finest achievements result from solving the most difficult problems. More than anything else, the making of a successful garden depends on responding creatively to the facts of the site. Very often, it is the difficulties of a site, not its amenities, that will, if handled correctly, result in the finest garden effects. And one of the more challenging and ultimately fruitful problems a gardener can face is sloping, even steeply sloping ground.

Although making a garden on a hillside can be challenging, at least one begins with one unquestioned asset: drama. The simple fact of the topography ensures that whatever else the garden achieves, it at least will not be boring. Of course, as perverse as humans often are, we fail sometimes to see our good fortune when it lies before us. My own garden is located in the mountains of Vermont, and is all on a hillside; not a single square foot of flat ground was here when I came. Yet rather than recognize how lucky I was, I cursed the slopes and tried to bulldoze them out of existence. Happy for me that the attempt was futile, certainly in intention, but more to the point, actually in execution. For the more flat land the bulldozer operator succeeded in whittling out of the hill for a backyard, the more precipitous its bordering slopes became. Finally, a combination of his frustration and the limits of my finances caused me to call a halt to his efforts. So instead of the boxwood parterres and brick paths I had imagined when I first looked out over the uncleared land, I have instead a garden that is a child of the land itself. It folds with gentle logic into a deep cleft carved by advancing glaciers eons ago, down to and up from where a little stream still runs a pretty course without much intervention from me. There are habitats for every plant I wish to grow, and as my knowledge increases, I discover new ones. The experience of moving through the garden, for me at least, is richly varied, and surprise lies around every ascent and turning of the path. I wonder now why I had craved a garden as flat and undifferentiated as a card table.

In making a hillside garden, it is important to remember that the experience of it will be far more active than that of gardens made on level ground. We must work harder to see the garden, pulling ourselves up the hillside against gravity and perhaps also against the weight of our advancing years. So several concerns are crucial if the experience of the garden is to be pleasing rather than merely taxing, a sort of tonic exercise more beneficial to the cardiovascular system than to the spirit. More than gardens on flat surfaces, a hillside garden should reward us amply for the extra trouble it has caused us. It should—by turnings and by the revelation of unexpected vistas—beckon us always forward. It should reveal itself only slowly, never allowing itself to be taken in at a glance, promising always that if we go a little farther, and a little farther still, unanticipated pleasures will be ours. At its best, the hillside garden should possess the magic of a mountain hike, where clearings beckon, where vegetation thins to promise magnificent outcroppings of rock, and where, finally, we have hope of reaching the top and surveying with pleasure the extent to which we have traversed.

Such is the emotional content possible to a hillside garden; from it follows the most important element in such a garden—its paths, for they will control our sense of the space as it unfolds before us. More perhaps than with access in other kinds of gardens, hillside paths must be very carefully planned. We cannot count, as is always the best way in relatively flat gardens, on the logic of feet, waiting to fashion our paths more or less according to the way we have instinctively traveled in our daily rounds. Rather, on steeply sloping ground we will have to carve access into the earth, imagining the way we would like to go if we could. Paths on sloping ground will perforce also often have to be more narrow than the general rule for paths—that they be wide enough for two people to walk abreast in easy conversation—since they must hug whatever narrow ribbon of flat land one is able to wrest from the slope. They are not the worse for that, for their constriction forces contemplation; but narrow as they must sometimes be, they must still be constructed in such a way as to guarantee sureness of foot; and it is well if they broaden out here and there to make landings where we can catch our breath, look back on the experience of where we've been, compare notes with a companion, real or imaginary, and prepare for what lies ahead.

Almost always, paths that traverse hillsides should travel along the sides of a slope rather than cut straight up through it. Where ascent of the slope is necessary, they should switch back and forth much like mountain roads or hiking trails, or perhaps they might wrap in a graceful curve around the belly of the slope and disappear at its crest. This both prevents the climb from seeming tortuously unnatural and avoids the construction of steps, which are both difficult to fashion in long flights and difficult to ascend. Wherever natural obstacles occur or may be convincingly placed, causing a path to deviate from its straight course—obstacles such as a large, half-buried rock, a tree, a massed group of shrubbery, or even a decaying stump—they should be seized on to keep the path from seeming unnaturally direct, which real paths in such a site never are. Nor should paths be multiplied across the face of a hill simply to give access to another bed or offer another way to go, unless one can be hidden from the other by dense, full-bodied shrubs that allow no views through. For even dumb beasts will find the one best way up a hill, and two ways—or more—defy the logic behind any ascent, which is to get to the top.

Between the switchbacks of a path or along its edges will lie beds that should be planted as densely as possible, inviting no shortcuts. They essentially will be mixed borders, containing small understory trees, deciduous and evergreen shrubs, ground covers, and bays here and there, sunny for special herbaceous perennials or shady for woodland

ferns and other treasures. Generally, the plantings along the paths of a hillside garden can be richer and more varied than plantings on level land, for hillside gardens by their very nature are of an ambling sort, able to accommodate more variety and surprise. Still, however, a greater attention should be paid to texture and to mass than to flower color, for the greater variety in topography will demand a greater emphasis on repose. Most crucial is that massed shrubs or small trees be placed on the lower edge of the slope, to cut against our sense of the rise of the hill, making the ascent seem less formidable. And although hillside gardens are best when treated with a seemingly semi-wild intention, the intro-duction of an occasional formal shape—a conical Alberta spruce, a strong, dark column of yew or a globe of boxwood—will give a necessary sense of order and discipline to other plantings.

As all paths must lead somewhere, at the top of the ascent there might be a little terrace cut into the hillside, backed by a retaining wall of dry stonework above and within which little alpines could be tucked, for the joke of suggesting that one had climbed above the tree line to find tiny plants that rewarded the closest observation. There might be a bench as well, on which one could sit and survey the garden below before beginning the descent. For there is magic in any lookout, a magic buried in our memory from the time when a view of things was crucial to our very survival.

Although it is the special emotional resonances of a hillside garden that will reward its owner for the labor of its making, certain practical considerations are also terribly important. Practically, there are three large concerns in installing a garden of this type. The first is drainage and the construction of footings that will keep the garden from slithering down into a heap under the pressure of unusually heavy rains. If you live in an area where mud slides are a problem, you will already know about the necessity of securing slopes from slippage; if you do not, then those in charge of your local construction ordinances certainly will. But in such places, it is crucial to secure the services of an engineer, and to be sure that all local requirements have been met. The consequence of failing to take these steps may at the least be heavy fines and some very expensive reconstruction, and at the worst of finding most of your garden inside the kitchen when you go down some morning to make coffee.

In areas where severe erosion and mud slides are not a concern, hillsides can be fashioned into pleasing gardens simply through the technique of cutting and banking, which may require the services of an excavator, or may be done with only a shovel and a lot of energy, depending on the ambitiousness of the project. To cut and bank, earth is cut from the side of a slope to form a letter L, the soil taken from within the letter piled below to form a sustaining bank. Additional earth is removed to make the vertical portion of the letter a pleasing slope, and it, too, is piled against the lower slope to gentle it. The result will be a gently descending ribbon along the slope where the path will be laid. But until vegetation roots firmly into the disturbed earth of the upper and lower slopes, they will be unstable and subject to erosion. It is therefore important to pack the earth firmly on both slopes, planting them thickly and mulching heavily. In cases where the upper slope cannot be gentled sufficiently to create stability and a pleasing configuration, the gardener may need to set a small retaining wall above the path line. In naturalistic hillside gardens, such walls should, if possible, be made of native stone, and laid without mortar so that small plants can be established in the crevices. Although the slopes that result from cutting and banking may look precipitous and unrestful at first, when the plants have blended together, they may, in fact, be barely perceptible.

Probably the most successful hillside gardens seem more the work of nature than of man, their paths suggesting ancient tracks first carved by foraging animals or by wanderers in the wilderness. For this reason, path surfaces of natural materials—of bark, gravel, or native flat stone—always seem to look best as paving for hillside paths. Brick or regular-patterned quarried stone laid in cement suggest, by their rigidity, an order imposed on the land rather than one dictated by it. And the sharp edges of such pavement never seem to blend successfully with the surrounding vegetation, or follow, in gentle falls and rises, the contours of the land.

Of course, an informal garden is not the only sort that could be brought into existence on sloping ground. The great continental tradition, particularly in Italy, works in a quite different fashion, establishing level terraces and parterres supported by grand retaining walls. Steps, when they occur, are broad, straight, and ceremonial, governed, as is all, by a strict geometry. It is a very aristocratic style of gardening, perhaps far from most suburban and even country homes in North America. With the right style of house—and the right kind of pocketbook—such an approach might certainly be the thing to try.

Water in the Garden

I do not live where I expected to. When I came to Vermont twenty years ago, it was in search of an old house. I had once rented one, outside Boston, that dated from 1753, and its old beams and fireplaces had come for me to signify place. But, in fact I now live in a new house (relatively new, for time passes, and it is now two decades old) and I don't at all regret it. Gardener that I am, I was seduced, on a pretty wooded hillside with not an old house or even a crumbling barn in sight. And it was not rich pastureland, ancient walls, or even two-hundred-year-old oaks that did it. It was water. A stream, bright and quick in the spring flood, fell the length of the property. I knew it was worth an antique fireplace.

I am not the first gardener to fall for water. The very idea of a garden is the child of water, of the oasis in the desert around which might be grown trees for shade and fruit. Every gardening tradition, whether of moist places like Japan or Northern Europe or dry ones, like Spain or Southern California, has celebrated water. It is at the heart of the great formal Renaissance gardens in Italy and France. It is equally essential to the tiny urban gardens of Kyoto and Tokyo. And those lucky enough to possess a pond or stream have already the very soul of their garden defined.

But if, in every garden, water is a delight, still it must be used sensitively. Not all water features are appropriate to all gardens. So, for example, a wildly bounding stream would not suit a garden of formal terraces and parterres, nor a Trevi fountain, however reduced in size and made in concrete, a modest cottage garden. Water in the garden must seem not only natural but inevitable, as if it had been there, predating the garden built around it.

Gardens that declare themselves to be unnatural, that depend upon formal axes, on stone-retained terraces and the patterns of geometry, should treat water in a similar fashion. There, the still, circular pool, the stone-coped water course, the lead tank, even the formal fountain, similarly announce and celebrate the ordering human hand. As such, they are in perfect harmony with the garden's intention.

By contrast, running streams (or dry ones), horse ponds, ditches, swamps, natural waterfalls, modest or grand, all bespeak an untrammeled nature into which humans have quietly insinuated their lives. And herein lies a difficulty. Where natural gardens are attempted in utterly man-made worlds—that is, in cities and suburbs—water is much harder to integrate in a believable fashion. In such gardens the suspension of disbelief is already hard enough, however sylvan and serene the garden itself manages to be, with the alley and its dumpster just beyond the fence, electric wires overhead, and the wail of fire trucks doing duty for the chirping of the chickadees. In such places, "natural gardens" are really something of a misnomer, and we must admit, however grudgingly, that there is no such thing. Gardens of any sort are wholly unnatural; they not only work to be something nature herself would never bring into existence, but they also strive to lie about the fact. Well done, the illusion of the natural garden can be quite convincing. Plants do, in fact, grow in most places, and they can be arranged in patterns drawn from nature's own practice, with the subtle difference—we hope for the better—that we did it, not she.

But in this sleight of hand we attempt to practice, water presents a special problem. It does not occur in most places, but only in very particular ones. For instance, it collects in low spots or in depressions hollowed out of rock basins by ancient glaciers. It does not often occur in deserts.

And in cities it feeds into storm drains, not into the creeks and rivers that once crisscrossed fields and forests but are now asphalted with streets and crowded with dwellings. So the little rill that rises up just at the corner of the garden where the stockade fence meets the brick wall of the apartment building next door, travels ten feet or so to collect in a little pond that never overflows its banks, strains credibility. Perhaps indeed there is a little fountain, powered by electricity, that can be shut on and

off at will. But however cleverly disguised, the whole contrivance will shout of recirculating pumps and plastic liners, in fact, of artifice.

Perhaps, then, even in the so-called natural garden, when we contrive a fact we ought just to admit it. Once, in a very beautiful garden as remarkable for its ingenuity as for its simplicity, I saw just such a frank admission of where the water was coming from and where it was going. Off in a corner, backed by some high shrubs, a mossy old cedar tub had been set under a water faucet, the tall sort that used to be in old-fashioned backyards for washing hands and face after garden chores were done, or to rinse soil from freshly pulled vegetables. Three large, flat stones led up to the tub, as if it still might be used—and perhaps was— for those practical purposes. But the faucet was allowed a constant, steady, gentle drip, just enough to keep the old tub full and barely over-flowing. All around it, in the constantly moist ground, throve bog-loving plants that could never have been coaxed to flourish in the open border. There were simple native ones—marsh marigolds, skunk cabbage, and the water forget-me-not, *Myosotis palustris*. But there were exotics, too, stately Japanese iris in cool blue and white, and *Primula* x *bullesiana,* the pale peach- and melon-colored candelabra primroses from the Himalayas. The effect was one of just the sort of honest beauty that all natural gardens should possess. Its lesson was that, except perhaps in the grandest natural gardens, water in gardens of that type should occur in such a way that even its origin can be frankly admitted. So, in many such gardens, a wooden tub, a large soapstone tank, or even an oversized clay pot of good design, with its drainage hole filled with a wine cork, can introduce the soothing presence of water, making possible the cultivation of an unusual aquatic plant—a variegated rush, a papyrus, a colony of water hyacinths, or the elegant water lettuce. In all such cases the pre-sumption is clear: The source of the water is the garden hose.

In formal gardens, or in any garden scheme that takes its character from domestic use, water may be introduced in a somewhat more elabo-rate way. This is still not to say that ponds, rills, or waterfalls that attempt to seem natural can ever be convincing, for always one is aware of the plastic liner, the mortar that holds the fall together, the artifice with which the coping stones have been placed, and the various pipes, tubes, and pumps that keep the whole thing going. Such effects—to be quite blunt about it—are only an inch away from gazing balls, a plaster mother duck with her file of babies behind, or a plywood image of a portly female gardener, bottom up, bloomers showing. The water features I have in mind, for formal gardens or for garden spaces devoted to domestic use, take their identity from architecture rather than from nature. They are frankly built, even ornamented, as dwellings are. So, in an entrance court, for example, a tank of brick or stucco might be placed against a house wall of similar materials, or a raised pool—perhaps high enough for comfortable seating, with a coping of good dressed stone or even tile—might stand to one side of a paved terrace. A formal perennial garden, edged round with yew against which two deep perennial beds were planted, might have as its centerpiece a rectangular pool, again raised above the level of the surrounding grass and planted with water lilies. Or an herb garden with two brick paths crossing in the center could have an elevated round pool, rather like an old farm well, where they meet. I can think of no cleverer way of contriving that effect than by burying a large cement sewage culvert, say four feet across and eight feet in length, halfway into the earth, rough-stuccoing its surface or veneering it with brick. In the right kind of vegetable garden, such a feature would also be magical, and convenient, too, for one could dip from it to water young seedlings or transplants, or maybe even grow, in submerged pots, a creditable crop of watercress.

All these examples emphasize one point. Unless it occurs naturally in a garden, water should be treated as an introduced element. Where it does occur naturally, it is to be treasured beyond all things. Where it does not, one does best always to admit that it has been brought in, never pretending that it was there from the start. For in gardens, as in poetry, beauty and truth are the same thing.

Sculpture in the Garden

The question to ask about sculpture is this: What role, if any, can it play in modern gardens? Historically, of course, it has been a part of gardens—the main part, perhaps—from classical times through the Renaissance. Roman gardens were essentially stage sets where architectural effects were contrived and sculpture set everywhere to manifest the taste, or at least the wealth, of the owner. Although we think of gardens as places to grow plants, for the Romans, living things played essentially architectural roles, clipped to form walls and arches or shaped into topiary obelisks, peacocks, pine cones, stags, and such. Plants thus became either vegetable masonry or statues in themselves. Renaissance gardens borrowed these effects from Rome and set about either unearthing the buried statues or copying them to grace the parterres, terraces, allées, and fountains of the garden. In both cases, although urns and obelisks existed in plenty, it was the human form, idealized as gods, goddesses, or subjects from mythology, that was most popular for garden ornament. Such ornamentation attracted attention to itself not only by being representations of the human figure, but of the human figure in a certain shapely amplitude and perfection of marbled flesh; whether arms were crossed in modesty or not, or a fallen fig leaf settled unaccountably just where it should be (or not), one naturally looked in that direction. Whether the effect was of an outdoor museum or frankly pornographic, plants played a secondary role against such garden ornament.

The great landscape gardens made in England by William Kent, Lancelot Brown, and Henry Hoare in the heart of the eighteenth century, although they eschewed generally the terraces, stairs, parterres, and long reflecting pools of the Italian style, nevertheless retained statuary and architectural ornament. The sweeping lawns punctuated by natural groupings of trees, the verdant woodland rides that amply invited the eye to distant mountain tops, the picturesque cows cunningly held at an attractive distance by ha-has, all were contrived to refer the landscape back to nature, albeit a "nature methodized" (as Pope would have it) by the controlling hand of man. Nevertheless, pictures of tranquil verdure were seen as just exactly that, *pictures,* requiring "point" from a temple, a ruined grotto, an imposing stature of Neptune (if there was water), or (if there were woods and lawns) of Apollo or Diana. Flora, when she, too, was invited in, was apt to be represented not by flowering plants grown in abandon, but by an attractive young woman whose modesty was satisfied more by garlands of roses than by sensible clothing.

Our gardens are different from all these. Perhaps because, unlike our ancestors, we live in a world where man is only too obviously master and nature but a remnant, modern gardens are usually simpler, more reverent attempts to celebrate nature's beauties as much as our own manipulation of them. In our gardens, it is plants that matter, first and last, and they matter for themselves, not as mere enhancements of other elements. Even the artificially created structures of the garden—its defining frame, its rooms, its paving—exist not for themselves, but rather to display the plants within them. Whether, therefore, many of the objects that are placed in modern gardens as pure ornament—gazing balls, plastic ducks, bloomered, bent-over grannies, or, more tastefully, renderings of eighteenth-century statues in stone, concrete, or imitation lead—are actually appropriate there is open to doubt.

Still, our gardens are, after all, *our* gardens, and we want to make them so by furnishing them with something of ourselves. So we stand benches and chairs in them, pots of annuals and tender plants summered out-of-doors, watering cans and wooden wheelbarrows. All these gentle marks of our presence and our caring can settle easily into the garden. These objects, after all, are part of the garden, essential to its life and our life in it. As they look so completely at home there, they suggest a general attitude toward objects used in the garden for decorative purposes.

Gardens are themselves artifacts, highly artificial manipulations of nature where the patterning of one plant against another makes beauty. To ask plants to compete with objects equally commanding—perhaps more commanding in their way—is to do a disservice both to plants and to objects. Both sculpture and the garden ask to be appreciated on their own terms, at least when they are good gardens and good sculpture. (When either—or even both—are bad, each might be helped out by the other, if only by way of distraction.) It is true that when gardens are designed specifically to display sculpture, the effect may be satisfying; but in such cases, it is always the sculpture that takes prominence, the plants being relegated to the roll of simple enhancement, as a backdrop—a curtain, a carpet, or the walls of a room. Very often native vegetation, subtly enhanced, and lots of grass provide all that is needed. And then, one is not so much in a garden as in an outdoor museum.

Sometimes, also, a specific piece of sculpture may be designed for an existing garden, much as a painting may be commissioned for a beautiful room. It is surprising how seldom such efforts are successful. But whatever the results, the approach has this advantage, that it will avoid the banality of mass-produced objects, usually in raw concrete or in some thin substance patinated to imitate lead or bronze or stone. And a piece of original modern sculpture will usually reflect the natural shapes of the garden—twig, tree, or rock—in its form, and even be made of material that will in time age as the garden does. Still, the ultimate success of such objects will depend in equal measure on their innate beauty, on the harmony with which they resonate with the garden as a whole, and on the tact with which they are mounted and placed. More than one such object has been moved restlessly about the garden, finally to settle beautifully in a field or in an unimproved bit of woodland—or even, lacking such places, to be sent back to its maker.

The great danger, of course, in siting sculpture of any sort in the garden is pretension. For unless an object adds to the inherent beauty of a garden by fitting perfectly into its scale and its overall intention, it will be seen as an ostentatious announcement of the size of the gardener's bank account or perhaps of the inordinate love he bears for his grandchildren, now cast forever in bronze. Worse even than the overscaled detritus of defunct wealthy estates, or family portraits fashioned in durable metals by modern "masters," are costly, mass-produced pieces that carry little in the way of either craft or beauty, but that were had for a price from mail-order catalogs. Gardens are always unique, the particular vision of the gardener who makes them. How sad, then, to see the originality of gardens trivialized by objects, for just the same money, that might appear at the local filling station. Put that little seated cement girl wherever you please in your garden; she will still be the same little girl we have seen dozens of times in other gardens, and she will still not have remembered where she left her clothes.

Generally, rather than looking for expensive or mass-produced objects to place about the garden, it is better to look to the garden itself for its ornament. A simple handsome stone, placed as a marker to a path; an oversized, well-proportioned clay pot, empty or planted to one choice specimen; a stone sink filled with saxifrages or other tiny alpine plants; a bit of architectural fragment, mossy and half lost in a bed of ivy; river stones of rounded shape piled by a gate or at the edge of a terrace; a birdbath made of a low-rimmed clay pot with a cork in its drainage hole; all these can serve to ornament the garden, adding point to a scene, focusing a view, or emphasizing a favorite spot. A bench or a seat in the garden is always nice, even if one never sits on it, simply for the possibility it offers (someday, when one has the time) and for the way it suggests that the garden is not merely to be looked at but lived in.

Perhaps the best of all garden ornaments are plants themselves. A great old tree, whether rugged of bole like an oak or wide-spreading like an apple, focuses any garden scene, forcing all the attendant plants around it into the service of its beauty. But lesser plants, ones that can reach maturity in several seasons—or even in one—can be thought of as elements of decoration. Any plant that is singular in its form, strong and striking in its outline, can serve as a sort of vegetable sculpture. The rigid column of an Irish yew, or of the much hardier *Taxus* x *media* 'Robusta' and 'Sentinel', can be placed at a partly sunny turn of a woodland ramble to give meaning to a hardly cultivated tumble of ferns, hostas, and wild woodland perennials. Alberta spruce, as neat as an old-fashioned conical drinking cup upside down, can almost never be misused once freed from its obligatory presence on either side of a front door. A single clump of prickly yucca, its upright swords surmounted by a dramatic candle of ivory flowers, may be enough for ornamentation in a stark, modern courtyard; alternately, many ornamental grasses, and particularly species of miscanthus, would serve there, or indeed, anywhere one wished a punctuating fountain of green or variegated foliage. And in winter, the fantastically contorted twigs and branches of *Corylus avelana* 'Contorta', called "Harry Lauder's walking stick," will provide far more fascination than a single shivering nymph in what looks to be lead.

It is interesting that most of the great theorists of garden design, although they all loved a bench or quiet seating place, were hostile to statuary and sculpture in the garden. Sir Francis Bacon, writing in 1625, comments that statues "are for state and magnificence; but nothing to the true pleasure . . . of a garden." Russell Page, writing more than three hundred years later in *The Education of a Gardener,* echoes Bacon's sentiment. "Flowers . . . are richness enough in the garden picture. To add further ornamentation is to distract."

Vegetable Gardens

If Louis Sullivan's often quoted dictum that "form follows function" is at all applicable to the design of gardens, it is certainly so where vegetables are grown. Unlike other parts of the garden, the vegetable plot exists first for purely practical purposes: to grow food. And whatever beauty a vegetable garden possesses must originate primarily from doing that task well.

So in thinking about the design and placement of a vegetable garden, one needs first to consider the requirements of the vegetables. There are few plants that are so exacting in their needs. Almost all food crops prefer a full day of sun in order to grow well. Even the so-called shade-tolerant crops—lettuce, spinach, and peas, for example—will flourish the better for growing in sun. The vegetable garden needs therefore to be put in the sunniest part of the property. Only heartbreak will result from compromise on this issue. And this is not all that vegetables ask. They also want the best soils, rich in organic matter, in phosphorus and potassium and in trace elements, neither too alkaline nor too acid. They want to be watered on a regular and frequent basis, either by evenly spaced rainfall or from the garden tap. They need both shelter from the wind and free air movement. They should not be grown in hollows or low places, for they are then subject to early and late frosts. And finally, most crops must be rotated annually, lest disease and insects specific to them build up in the soil.

All these needs determine the placement of the vegetable garden, but not its design. That is influenced most by the obvious fact that vegetable crops of one sort or another are generally grown together, all of one variety of lettuce here, cabbages there. So there is necessarily about the vegetable garden a sense of order and of logic that marks it off from the usually more seeming spontaneity of perennials and shrubs grown elsewhere in the garden. There is, however, a movement in American gardening that recognizes vegetables for the beautiful plants they are, and that strives to incorporate them into more purely decorative plantings. The results can be refreshingly startling, and sometimes very beautiful; whether placing the aesthetic characteristics of vegetable plants over their primary purpose as food results in better vegatables, however, is in doubt. There is the problem, too, of how to fill the gap in the perennial border when that fine purple cabbage reaches maturity and is required in the kitchen, an issue that does not generally arise with a Bergenia. The needs of vegetables and of perennials are also often not the same; one spaces differently, prepares the soil in a different way, uses—when they are necessary—different sprays and chemicals. But more than all these problems is the fact that gardens gain in complexity and beauty when they are seen as separate rooms, each devoted to its own purposes and each offering its own aesthetic pleasures. Both perennial and vegetable gardens are so different in effect—and each so wonderful—that blurring their distinctions may be more loss than gain.

Another characteristic of the vegetable garden that influences its design is the fact that vegetables are, for almost half the year, not there. Except in the mildest parts of the country, the ground lies fallow from November to March, tenanted, if at all, by a lonely row of brussels sprouts or hardy kale. So if it is to add beauty as well as food to the gardener's life, that beauty will depend on other elements—on its enclosure, its paths, its fallow, well-dressed rows, on the pattern it describes on the ground. Vegetable gardens organized as formal compositions have been traditional in both England and America since the seventeenth century, although their origins go much farther back than that, to the monastery gardens of medieval Europe, where "herbs and simples" were grown. In fact, the recent vogue for laying out vegetable gardens as a series of artfully arranged beds—"potagers," as it is presently fashionable to call them—is a return to practices common centuries ago. The vegetable garden at Mount Vernon was, and remains, one of the finest examples in this country of such a garden. Despite its grand scale, it is a model to follow in the design of far more modest vegetable gardens. That design is eminently practical, but also very beautiful. And when any garden effect, any arrangement of plants, has been around for a long, long time, it will carry with it always the faint perfume of other times, other ways of living; and that is, for many gardeners, one of the primary reasons for gardening, providing them with a living link to the past.

The first requirement of the formal vegetable garden—as, I would argue, of all gardens—is enclosure. But it may be true about vegetable gardens, more than of any other sort, that they demand some sort of structure that sets them apart. In the beginning, a stout wall or fence was a practical necessity (and may still be), as it protected food crops from the depredations of domestic or wild animals, and created a microclimate in which plants could be brought early to productive maturity. Beyond that, however, a vegetable garden is so particular in its needs and so pronounced in its character that it is good to set it off as a world apart, one possessed of its own emotional resonances. When one weeds, also—as, in a vegetable garden one must relentlessly—it is pleasant to know exactly where one's labors stop.

I have seen vegetable gardens hedged round with elegant clipped walls of yew or arborvitae, and if one has lots of space at one's command, their somber dignity makes anything, even bare ground, beautiful. Generally, however, fencing is preferable to hedging as a vegetable garden's defining parameters. For hedges block the flow of air, and its free movement is a powerful aid in keeping down many diseases, particularly mildew. Also, one cannot plant too near a hedge, since it will cast shade and its roots will compete for nutrients and moisture with vegetable crops. The advantages of fencing are both that these problems are eliminated, and also that the fence itself can support crops. Annual vegetables such as beans, peas, cucumbers, and tomatoes can be trained against it, and permanent plants—espaliered apples and pears, raspberries and blackberries, fan-trained blueberries, gooseberries, and currants—will provide not only delectable fruits in season, but also interesting structures when the garden is dormant. My own vegetable garden is surrounded by split-rail locust fencing, gray, irregular, and craggy, appropriate to its rural Vermont setting. In suburban gardens, white or gray picket fencing might serve better, and in California, nothing would be nicer than a rustic fence

of grape stakes. Fencing of solid work—board or stockade or even elegant brick—should be avoided on most properties, both because of the blockage of airflow, and because the vegetable garden, despite its strong character, should be admitted into the general garden picture, integrated with it, if only by a tantalizing glimpse.

The second necessity in designing a vegetable garden for all-season beauty is pathing, since whatever patterns the garden makes upon the earth are strengthened by paths, and in autumn, winter, or early spring, they may be its essential internal structure. The paths of my own garden are of flat granite fieldstone, since that is what the land offered. But brick could do as well, or—for a lot more money—handsome plates of cut bluestone. Even gravel, if it is well-coped to prevent it from migrating into the rows, could be very satisfying, pleasant underfoot and a great pleasure, after the day's weeding is done, to rake smooth. But whatever pathing is chosen for the vegetable garden, it should be of a hard and permanent material, both for the beauty of its surface and because so much of the time spent in a vegetable garden is spent in damp weather.

When considering permanent pathing, it will occur to many gardeners that it will be rather difficult to manipulate the rototiller through the space. But in the maintenance of a vegetable garden, rototilling is a much overvalued activity, perhaps because as one *did* ask for so expensive and so large a thing for Christmas, one had better use it. Power tillers are very useful—almost necessary—in the opening up of new land for the cultivation of vegetables, and so are worth renting. But in the maintenance of an established vegetable plot, one well-maintained by annual additions of humus in the form of manure and good homemade compost, their uses are very limited. Further, they destroy the bed definitions of the garden, requiring a laborious refiguring of its space each year with stakes and a spool of twine. The establishment of permanent plants, whether raspberries, rhubarb, asparagus, strawberries, or elegant espaliers and standards, will be much more difficult. One must place them all at the edges, where visually much of their value may be lost. Far better to have recourse to the garden spade, turning compost in and making the deep, crisp row lines that only the hand and eye can fashion. It is satisfying work, bringing one into intimate contact with the earth and its needs;

and if one's soil is so compacted that it needs a power tiller to break through it, then one would do better to add an extra layer of compost next autumn, for that is not soil in which vegetables can be expected to thrive.

The paths of a vegetable garden ought probably to be straight, true to the rows and beds, dividing the garden in two, or forming a cruciform pattern that separates it into quarters. It is always pleasant if major paths end in some feature, a bench on which to sit, or in larger spaces, a pergola of grapes under the shade of which one can rest. Lesser paths, particularly if they end, as they should, against the defining frame of the garden, might simply justify traveling that way by a water butt, or even a handsome espalier against the fence. But any garden path should reward one with something special at the end, and this is as true in a vegetable garden as anywhere else. Otherwise, one turns around to traverse the length again, unsatisfied.

And the beds themselves, what shapes ought they to assume? It is certainly true that some crops will always do best when grown in rather long rows. Peas, for example, require supports of chicken wire or net strung on sturdy posts, an almost impossible thing to do if one does not have a straight shot at it. Corn, the undisputed queen of the August garden, certainly looks splendid grown in isolated towers of leaf, but to produce a good crop, it requires being grown in close rows so that the pollen of its tassels can fall on the silk of the ears below. Once one begins making rows, however, it is very easy to get trapped in that satisfying pattern and the consequence—putting aside a certain monotony—may be that one will tend to grow far too much of some crops, beans, for example, simply because the length of the row is there and the seed is in one's hand. Pretty things can be done with swirls, circles, and half-moons, and that might be tried for a season or two. But vegetable plants are often rather unruly, and although they may sometimes be propped into order with twigs or tied back with strings, they will tend to destroy elaborate patterns and be far more difficult to cultivate. In the long run, then, rectilinear shapes serve best, although the most practical arrangement may be a series of long rows punctuated by smaller beds of a square or rectangular shape. In such beds, taller, slower-maturing crops such as cabbage or potatoes can be grown in the center, the edges planted to lettuce, green onions, leeks, bush beans, or (where the center crop may be expected to mature to the edges of the beds) quick-developing vegetables such as radishes, salad rocket, miner's lettuce, or lambs' quarters. For additional interest, especially in the depths of winter, small standard trees of currant or gooseberry might be planted in the center of each bed, or, simply for their beautiful August flowers, standards of *Hydrangea paniculata* 'Grandiflora', which blooms on new wood and so can be trimmed quite tight.

Although the first requirement of any vegetable garden ought always to be that it produces vegetables, it should not be thought of merely as a utilitarian, practical space. Except with the most committed vegetable gardeners (who are often not interested in growing anything else), the result of such thinking can too often be that the vegetable plot will become the poor stepchild of the garden as a whole—weedy, ill-tended, perhaps productive, but not very nice to be in. One spends so much time working in a vegetable garden, and it is sometimes such a pleasant retreat from the world, or even from other cares in the garden, that it ought to be as beautiful as possible. Even flowers might be grown there, especially those wonderful ones that are too brash in color to compose well elsewhere. Loving *Lychnis chalcedonica,* a hardy perennial, for its uncompromising flowers of flame red, I found a place for it among the rows of 'Black Seeded Simpson' lettuce, where it glows splendidly. I have not grown zinnias since childhood, although the memory of them then and their wonderful cheerfulness endears them to me. So, next year in the vegetable garden, there might be a row, for picking and for the sheer pleasure of weeding among them. Why not?

Children in the Garden

As work is what chiefly defines an adult's day, so play defines a child's. For children, everything about the world is new. The work of their days is trying out the baffling and delightful plethora of possibilities that lie before them. Gardening is one of those, and children, watching their parents go about it, want to do it, too. But what the child wants—needs—to do is not quite the same thing the parents are bent on achieving. Adults work in the garden to secure a certain order, a pleasing pattern of plants, stone, carpenter's work, and water. The effort is directed to making something beautiful that, once achieved, can be contemplated and enjoyed. But for children, what matters much more is experiencing the process, playing at the rituals and rhythms of gardening, *doing* things. The product, be it a pleasing bed of bright annuals, a bountiful crop of tomatoes, a towering delphinium or a great, fat watermelon, is less immediately the point. Or rather, it is a separate point, only tangentially connected to the process that brought such results into being. The work itself is initially the point, work that the child perceives as play, albeit very serious play, as all true play is. Having done one thing, the child wants to do another, and after that, another still. Everything is process, change, experiment.

I have a friend of many years who began gardening at the age of three. His grandmother gave him a single rhizome of bearded iris. It was a pet iris, really, which he delighted in moving around the garden on an almost daily basis. Finally it came to rest in the tunnel of an overgrown privet hedge, a secret hiding place just big enough for him. And for his companionable iris.

The grandmother of this child (who now, in his maturity, is a distinguished gardener) must have been keenly observant, both about gardening and about the ways of children. For few other plants would have stood such treatment, and such treatment is, of course, just what would delight a very small child. The iris never bloomed; neither did it die outright, at least not until the child finally abandoned it in its privet gloom to turn to other pursuits. It survived long enough to provide his first lesson in gardening, that plants are gentle, patient things that mostly will not hurt you, and that will, with an increase of knowledge and skill, give abundant satisfaction, none ever better perhaps than a special sort of companionship.

As much as children like to move things about, they like to make messes. For them, there is a keen sensual pleasure in playing in the dirt. Making mud, discovering all the wonderful creepy things that live in the earth, digging holes and poking things into them, all these are a large part of what makes working in the garden seem like great fun on a Saturday morning. What for an adult may be merely labor necessary to achieve results is for the child often the greatest part of the pleasure. Pity the child gardener who is not allowed to get gloriously dirty, whose sneakers must remain pristinely white and whose jeans must look at midday still crisp from the laundry. For children are much closer to the dirt than are adults, almost, as parents know, to the point of thinking of it as their natural element. So it is that the true gardener's life, as all life did, we are told, begins in a magical combination of earth and water—a mess.

That children go at gardening with purposes somewhat different from those of adults means that if you are gardening with a child, it is probably best to give them their own plot to work in. There they can do pretty much as they please, with gentle guidance, never disturbing the plan of the garden as a whole or the adult's wishes for it. And nothing really is nicer for both parent and child than providing the child with his or her own separate space to garden, fenced or hedged perhaps, or even tucked out of sight behind the garage. Unsightly but important experiments can thus be kept out of the general view. But more important, such a sequestered space gives the child two emotional commodities precious to all children: privacy, and a sense of unfettered ownership, of sole posses- sion. The sense of independence—of empowerment—that results will further the concern all adults must have who are entrusted with the care of children—that they be given early the equipment essential to becom- ing adults in their own time.

This is not, of course, to say that the child's first efforts at gardening should occur in a sort of backyard Siberia. For although giving a child his or her own place to garden is the first part of the education of a gardener, it is just as important to garden *with* them. In the beginning, the child's whole sense of gardening will be to emulate what you are doing. If you are growing vegetables, the child will want to grow them, too. If there is a trellis in your garden, then there had best be one in the child's garden also. If you have a wheelbarrow or a compost bin, then child-sized ver- sions of these are also likely to be required. Conversely, if your whole sense of gardening is cutting the grass, your child will be no more sophis- ticated, and will tire of that chore as quickly as you do, probably more quickly. Nothing, perhaps, requires greater tact than varying the tasks of the garden according to the child's waxing or waning interest. And most certainly the last way to involve children in gardening is to view them as free labor, or to set them to tasks beyond their patience in the mistaken notion that character will therefore be developed. More likely you will develop boredom instead, and a lifelong aversion to gardening itself.

Perhaps generally the hardest part of gardening for children is the patience it requires. The ability to anticipate the future is essential in growing plants. Even the simple radish needs its thirty days to perform the miracle of its fat, red, edible ball. Other vegetables and flowers take much longer, and trees and shrubs longer still. Children live in a different sense of time than adults do, however, and the opportunity to see past, present, and future in a single plant—although it comes to be one of the deepest pleasures of gardening—is largely closed to them. For them, a sin-

gle summer is a significant faction of their whole life, and next year is an almost incomprehensible concept. Literally, they cannot wait. So if their interest in gardening is to grow, things need to happen rather fast. And sometimes a little tactful deceit on the part of parents is just what is needed. My sister, when she was a very little girl, fell in love with watermelons. She liked eating them, of course, and spitting the seeds at me. But it was really their satisfying shapes that won her, as big as she and much too heavy to carry. So my parents made her a bed beside the roses and she and they planted a hill of watermelon seeds. The seeds sprouted quickly, and the vines grew rampantly in the heat of a south Jersey summer. But the fruits were months away when her impatience began to turn first to frustration and then to indifference. It was at that point that my father intervened, early one morning, sneaking in not a single melon, but three huge ones bought from the local fruit stand. My sister woke to ecstasy, and has been hooked for life on the joys of gardening.

It is, I suppose, always easy for adults to condescend to children, to assume that because they are small and young, they are incapable of subtlety and discrimination. Adults always seem to assume that children will want to grow only what is big and brightly colored and odd—sunflowers, cabbage trees, luffa gourds, marigolds, zinnias, and fire-engine red pelargoniums. Children will, of course, delight in these plants, all excellent and joyful in their way, and new to them as most else is. But they might as much enjoy the fragrance of a rose, the intricate patterning of an agave, the hidden beauty of the codonopsis bells that must be gently lifted up to peer into. In the long run, then, much is gained by sharing with children not only the simpler beauties of flowers, but also their subtlety and complexity, an appreciation of which provides the enduring pleasure of gardening for a whole life. For the joy children take in gardening is not merely childish joy, something to be put away when more sophisticated pleasures come with the advance of years. And the surest way to understand a child's interest in gardening is to look deeply into one's own. Adults also need their secret places, their private havens from the world, their pride of possession. Come spring, plunging one's hands deep into moist earth is good at any age, a positive longing, an appetite in itself. Fat worms are always to be greeted with pleasure, and slugs with an "ugh" of disgust. A flower that opens for the first time from seed we have sown is as thrilling at sixty as it was at six.

Gardening successfully with children gives them a gift and a solace that will last longer than any other we can provide. But it also reminds us of why we started gardening in the first place, and why it matters, and why—past childhood in the chronological sense—we still do it. The gift, then, goes both ways.

Greenhouses: The Winter Garden

*F*or most gardeners, the pleasures of winter are largely compensatory. Skiing, wood fires, late rising, and slow-cooking soups and stews are nice enough, but hardly equal to a fresh June morning in the garden. Some gardeners are, of course, lucky enough to live where winter is a relatively mild affair. For them, the camellias, witch hazels, hellebores, cyclamen, and all other plants that want to blossom in the darkest months will do so with little assistance from the gardener. But for the rest of us, who live where winter steals the garden away, where the ground freezes hard and temperatures fall well below zero or hover just above, having flowers in winter—what is aptly called the "dead" of winter—requires some contrivance.

Visitors from England often comment on how few American gardeners have greenhouses and conservatories. In England, they are ubiquitous, attached to the most modest of homes or tucked at the back of cottage gardens near the "veggies." But here in America, enclosures for growing plants in winter are thought of as adjuncts to great estates, or perhaps as the indulgence of the truly mad gardener. Part of the fault for this lies, I suspect, in the American fascination with gadgetry. A greenhouse or conservatory is really a simple affair. It is just a shed with lots of glass and enough heat to keep out the worst chill of winter. But many American gardeners suppose that a successful greenhouse requires ugly aluminum framing, automatic ventilators, temperature alarms, humidifying systems, and elaborate plumbing of all sorts. Commercial greenhouses, and those devoted to the cultivation of specialty plants—orchids, rare jungle bromiliads, or desert cacti—do require such elaborate contrivances. But a home greenhouse—if it is to be primarily a place to putter through the winter, to enjoy the smell of the earth and the sight of flowers made more precious by their scarcity, perhaps to store a few tender shrubs in pots for summer decoration—can be fitted out of far simpler and less costly materials. In fact, it need not even be a greenhouse at all.

Twenty years ago, on first coming to live in Vermont, I rented a rambling old farmhouse with a large, south-facing glassed-in porch. Such porches are common features of older Vermont houses, where they are known as "drying rooms" and provided places to hang the laundry in winter long before the questionable convenience of the electric dryer was invented. They are usually (as was mine) long galleries with three or so feet of uninsulated wall above a wooden floor, and banks of small-paned windows—simple barn sash windows—running along the three exposed sides. Unless they have been modernized, their only source of heat is the sun, and perhaps such warmth as might escape from the house itself or from a door left open. Even bare, or perhaps hung with a portion of the family's wash, they are wonderful spaces. The house I rented had other amenities, and the patina of almost two hundred years of human life within it. But I put down my deposit and moved in, I am sure, just because of that porch. For I knew it would provide a space for a collection of plants, and for a happy winter of experiments new to me and eagerly anticipated.

Still, I doubt I would have succeeded with any of them had I not taken a lesson from my new Vermont neighbors. As they did, I piled bales of hay against the foundation of the porch, to block the icy wind that swept beneath it and to trap the insulating snow. I found—a great piece of luck—a complete additional set of barn sash windows in the back of the old barn, dusty, in need of repair and a fresh coat of paint, but enough to provide an extra layer of outer glazing for additional insulation. From old boards in the barn loft I made staging against the outer walls, crude free-standing bleachers on which pots could be stood in three tiers.

In autumn, just before frost, I moved in a collection of plants I had accumulated in my Boston apartment, nothing very choice, only the ficus tree everyone seems to acquire at some point, a calamondin orange, a collection of potted ivies, a pseudo bonsai of juniper, and a dreary but serviceable aspidistra. All that summer I had grown Korean chrysanthemums into mop-headed standards, and I potted up pachysandra and myrtle from around the foundations of the house, both pretty and undemanding plants for the shadier sections of cool conservatories. Although inexperienced in the rigors of a Vermont winter, I knew that my space was no place to grow choice orchids and tropical palms. But by then I had found my way to Allen Haskell's wonderful nursery in New Bedford, Massachusetts, and he steered me toward plants that would flourish and even bloom in quite cool conditions, the winsome blue felicia, geraniums scented of peppermint, nutmeg, and lemon, an elegant standard rosemary. From him I also bought a large, fat English boxwood (since, the mother of all the English box that now grow outdoors in our garden) that I put in a good clay pot to stand beside the open living-room door. I had read in T. H. Everett's *Illustrated Encyclopedia of Gardening* that many annuals thrive unexpectedly well in cool conditions and will bloom in winter, so I started some seed of salpiglosis in mixed colors and fantastic veining, and even three sickly seedlings of the beautiful yellow Mexican horned poppy, *Hunnemania fumariefolia*. Following Thalassa Crusoe's sound advice in *Making Things Grow*, I potted up a succession of bulbs for late winter flowering, just about everything, and too many, really—paperwhites, of course, and other narcissus, tulips, hyacinths, grape hyacinths, scyllas, and even a single fat bulb of *Fritillaria imperialis*. Just as she said I would, I got an incredibly long display from a single scarlet florist's cyclamen, vivid against my pachysandra and myrtle. Suddenly my porch, now a proper "plant room," was much smaller than I had supposed.

Despite its undeniable silent beauty and the opportunities it provides for sport of all sorts, no one could say that a winter in Vermont is an easy thing to get through, especially if it is one's first. I suffered from the cold, and from the unending snow. I missed Boston dreadfully, its movies, its shops and restaurants, its teeming streets. But I found compensation, great indeed, from my first experiments at winter gardening. There were times when water, spilled from watering the pots, was frozen on the floor in the morning. Heating costs must have been horrific; I hardly know, although the living-room door had to be left open on the coldest nights and even on dark snowy days, and the furnace seems in my memory always to have been on. Not everything flourished, either. The *Fritillaria imperialis* was a bust, and a good thing, too, as I later learned, for it smells of something between skunk and rancid onion; the hunnemania, which Everett promised would produce "a long succession of bloom in late winter and spring from seed sown in August or September" produced only three, one apiece per plant, and not even in succession, but all three on a single blizzardy day. Still, there were flowers aplenty, and the plants flour-

ished in the quite cool conditions, even to the surprise of Allen Haskell, who came up to see. The simplicity of that porch and the pleasures I drew from it hooked me on winter gardening, as it must be understood in Vermont. After twenty years, it is in part why I am still here.

So when, two years later, I built my house, some sort of space for gardening in winter was a first necessity, more important than a garage or even finished flooring on the second story. Even from first dreaming, the house I imagined was to have a winter garden, built in its simple post-and-beam fashion and glazed with readily available materials, sheets of tempered glass hung double with an airspace between. It was to be open to the living earth—to the builder's despair—just so shrubs and small trees could be planted in the ground, and so I, on a cold February morning, could feel the soil and smell it. Although it faces south to catch all the sun that winter offers, it differs from my first plant room in that its floor is earth, it has glazing on the roof and a series of baseboard radiators against the outer walls, just enough to keep the frost out. It also opens on the kitchen, as it ought, for in winter in Vermont the kitchen is where one mostly is. Nor is there any staging for potted plants (as there had been originally), for it became apparent, after five or so years of living here, that a real garden, however small, would mean more than a collection of pot-grown plants arrayed on benches. So the ficus, the calamondin orange, the juniper bonsai are only memories now, having been replaced by a collection of camellias growing in the earth, a beautiful *Leptospermum scoparium* 'Ruby Glow', some tender rhododendrons for late-winter flowering, and Nancy Goodwin's lovely seed-grown hardy cyclamen (not "hardy," alas, for us outdoors, though we try and try) clustered along the fieldstone path that traverses the length of the space. Ask me if I would like it larger, and I will, of course, say yes, for there are so many winter-flowering shrubs, trees, and perennials that flourish at temperatures a few degrees above freezing that I would love to grow. Greenhouses and conservatories should be made of rubber, to expand with the gardener's interests, although that technology is not yet in place, and wouldn't be very attractive if it were.

The point of it all is this: All gardeners, wherever they live, sooner or later long for plants that cannot be cultivated in the garden outdoors, even if the climate enjoyed there is relatively mild. In some places—and I live in one—there may actually *be* no garden in winter, whatever delights may be offered by the stern, snow-laden outlines of conifers or the bright twigs of shrubby dogwoods. The passionate cultivation of plants and of flowers must then retreat indoors, even to the proverbial "sunny windowsill," although show me a gardener who has not long since outgrown the few of those that may be and I'll show you no gardener at all. Some sort of enclosed and heated growing space becomes one of the most precious assets a gardener can possess. It need not be very elaborate, need not—indeed, *should* not—be heated to tropical warmth, and it needs only those mechanical conveniences that genuinely amuse their owners and make life easier. I did very well on my simple plant porch, and I think now, with perhaps a kerosene space heater for the coldest nights, I could do even better. Some things I have never grown so well since, and actually I will always miss that space, for the beauty of its structure and its forthright country charm made the plants I grew there look all the better. Something like it would be easy to duplicate, for the carpentry was not complicated, and barn sash windows are still the cheapest and the most accessible glazing one can buy. Simple structures, built by a local carpenter or resident handyperson, can be fitted to almost any house, suiting it better perhaps than the kit greenhouses of aluminum and prefabricated glazing, although those, if one wishes to specialize in orchids or bromiliads or cacti in a big way, may still be the better choice. We grant, however, that although the gardener is prepared to move earth and even heaven in his pursuit of the love of plants, good gardening is still a matter of taking what one is given and making the most of it. So if one has a cold sunporch, or a scrap of winter garden open to the ground, one grows in it what will grow well there, just as out-of-doors. And one is content. For a time.

Utility Areas

*I*f it is true, as Alexander Pope said, that the art of gardening consists first in consulting the genius of the place, what are we to do when that genius is not a pond or a lichen-covered outcrop of granite or a stately ancient oak, but rather a collection of trash cans, the run for the family dog, or a basket of wet laundry? What we usually try to do is tuck such necessities away, with a shrug at their unsightly utility and a hope that behind the garage or back by the alley their unkempt clutter will not intrude too much on the more civilized parts of the garden. But a drying yard, a dog pen, or even the trash receptacles need not be a blemish on the face of the garden; they can be integrated into it, fashioned so that they enhance the beauty of the place and even offer a habitat for plants or pleasurable effects nowhere else possible.

The first requirement in making attractive these purely practical utility areas is to enclose them. Here, as in the more purely ornamental parts of the garden, enclosure organizes and defines a space. And if the thing enclosed is itself not particularly attractive, at least the enclosure can be.

The type of enclosure depends upon its purpose, though, as elsewhere in the garden, if a solution both solves a problem and also creates an amenity, so much the better. If the problem is simply to hide the trash cans or clothesline from view, then a simple wooden fence, trelliswork, or hedging will be all that is required. A hedge, if it is well-tended, properly fed, and trimmed, will be beautiful in itself, concealing what is behind and offering a quiet screen of somber green for a perennial border or a collection of choice dwarf shrubs and foliage plants before.

Always, with a hedge, great care must be taken in selecting the plants that will make it up. For utility areas, it is usually best to choose plants that will provide a crisp, tailored appearance, and so they must be amenable to tight shearing. Although healthy, well-trimmed hedges of privet or beech or hornbeam can be wonderful elsewhere in the garden, evergreens seem best as hedging for utility areas, since one doesn't want to look in winter at what one wanted to conceal in summer. It is important, too, to remember that the pleasure of a hedge lies in its uniformity, and so, if the site offers a variety of growing conditions—full sun at one end, dappled or deep shade at the other—plants should be selected that are capable of growing well throughout this range. Or, in such cases, perhaps it is better to opt for a fence or trellis.

Fences and trellises offer quite different possibilities from hedges, the best of which is that they provide space for many of the plants gardeners long to grow, and particularly for vines. So on a trellis or fence one can cultivate a collection of clematis, or wonderful noninvasive honeysuckles, or the cream-and-pink-splashed *Actinidia kolomitka,* or the elegant climbing hydrangea (*Hydrangea anomala petiolaris*). There might also be room for annual vines, from morning glories and scarlet runner beans to more exotic specimens such as *Rodochiton atrosanguineum* or the silver-variegated annual hop, *Humulus japonicus.* Both fences and trellises also provide a place for espaliers, for almost any woody plant one has no other space for in the garden can be trained flat—formally or informally—to provide an extra tier of bloom and a special effect. In fact, many plants such as flowering quinces and spireas—plants that usually offer little beyond a brief period of glorious bloom—can gain distinction throughout the gardening year by being treated as espaliers. Where there is full sun against the fence or trellis, nothing perhaps is more elegant than classically trained espaliers of apple or pear, either bought "ready-made" or trained from one-year grafted whips. But even part shade can be used to espalier fruits, although in that case one would choose blueberries, trained into fan shapes, or raspberries, tied in against the support.

But if an enclosure needs to wall something in or something out—as, for example, an overexuberant family pet—then hedges and even light fences and trellises will not serve. In such cases, the fence had better be of strong wood, or even of woven wire or chain link. Most gardeners would turn to wire fences as a last desperate resort, or they inherit them, despairingly, with the place. But even chain link, sturdily indefensible as it is generally thought to be, can be made beautiful. It may be painted dark green or black, and vines can be woven through it so that it becomes a sort of hybrid between a fence and a hedge, what one might call a "fedge." Perhaps the most elegant plant for creating this effect is English ivy in some plain green cultivar, of which, in cold climates, 'Baltica' would be the best. But other vines, if they remain thickly leaved from bottom to top, might also serve; even shrubs that are lax and whippy of growth, such as forsythia or flowering quince, can be woven with patience through a wire or chain-link fence. And once I saw a startlingly beautiful example of this effect, consisting of a procumbent, ground-hugging juniper that had been woven upward to the top of the fence and then allowed to weep downward in graceful tiers and swags. But in this attempt to make a silk purse out of a sow's ear, gardeners will perhaps think of other plants they would like to grow that could be grown in this way. *Hydrangea anomala petiolaris,* for example, would form thick muscular stems clad in strips of warm, brown, exfoliating bark through the winter, and its tiered growth would terminate in panicles of cream-colored, fragrant flowers in early summer. Although it is deciduous, it could be woven thickly enough through a wire fence to conceal or baffle what lay behind, even in winter. Alternately, there may be no other place to grow Hall's honeysuckle—pretty in growth and leaf and gorgeous in the scent of its white flowers fading to antique ivory—than a chain-link fence. It seems to have a natural affinity for such a support, and if it is bordered by mown grass, the one bad thing about the plant is taken care of, for it is fearfully invasive. And finally, among invasive plants—assuming always a mown strip of grass in front—something wonderful hap-

pens to a chain-link fence when it is planted to a hardy running bamboo, the feathery tall *Phyllostachys aureosulcata* or the wider-leaved, more tropical-looking *Sasa japonica* for first choices.

With utility areas, the gardener's first concern is naturally to conceal what lies within or behind. But it is just as important to be sure that the area being concealed is pleasant to enter, neat and tidy, certainly, and if possible even beautiful in a practical sort of way. It is all too easy to accept mess and disorder if it is nicely hidden from view, for what is out of sight, in the garden as elsewhere in life, can be comfortably out of mind. But one makes daily trips into—or at least past—most utility areas, and so it is reasonable to ask that they be as attractive inside as they may be made to be without.

Nothing makes a utility area pleasant to be in quite so effectively as a uniform ground surface, whether of clean-raked sand, gravel, field- or cobblestone, or wooden decking. As obvious as that point might be, it is one that I learned by accident. Behind the lower greenhouse at North Hill is an area we call the stock yard. There we stand the pots of new plants we have bought, more with an eye to their desirability than to any sense of where they might be planted in the garden. Also in this area are five cold frames, where some almost-hardy plants are stored for the winter, as well as the inevitable clutter of empty pots and plastic flats waiting to be returned to the nurseries for recycling. Until recently, this area was a difficult place for us to be, since the sight of so many much-desired plants still in their pots in July called up guilt and panic in about equal measures. Adding to the general sense of things out of control was an abundant growth of weeds, snuggling between the pots and nourished by the bare dirt and the daily watering required by our treasures. The area was certainly one to hide from visitors, and from ourselves as much as we could. So it was concealed by an eight-foot-tall board fence, painted a dark charcoal gray to match the siding of the greenhouse shop, with two gates of unpainted cedar providing access from either side. From the outside, there was instant improvement, although within, the same chaos reigned as before.

For another project, the remulching of the rock garden, we ordered a dump-truck load of pea stone. There is, as it happens, a lot of pea stone in a dump-truck load, and after the rock garden was finished, we found ourselves with a mountain of the stuff and no place to put it. So, like so many things that happen in a garden, accident turned to advantage. We moved aside the pots of the stock yard, stripped the earth of weeds, put down landscape cloth, and barrowed the excess stone into the stock yard. Immediately our attitude toward the space was transformed, for the surface was easy to rake clean, crunchy underfoot, and the pots could be arranged in neat rows against the sides of the cold frames, convenient to water and easy to shop among when the rare space appeared in the border, asking for an interesting new plant. What had been a hard place for us to be in actually became a pleasure to visit and to tend. Now we find ourselves swinging open the gates into the high wooden fence that surrounds the yard, once a compelling necessity and now a pleasant frame, inviting guests inside to admire our new acquisitions and to give advice on their culture and their eventual placement in the garden.

The marriage of beauty and utility, perhaps fundamental to all aesthetic achievement, is offered a rare chance at expression in those areas of the garden we usually consign merely to the practical business of living. So a drying yard, geometrically arranged, surrounded perhaps by a high, airy trellis on which beautiful vines are trained, can be as satisfying as a fine formal garden. The daily trip to the garbage cans may be an opportunity to admire the stone paving of a path, to check on the progress of an espalier against a concealing fence, rich with ripening apples, to take pleasure in a clump or two of hosta luxuriating in the shelter of their galvanized guardians. We may feel better about consigning the family dog to his daytime confinement, as we go off to work, if the yard made for him is fedged with English ivy, cleanly surfaced with gravel, and half-shaded, for his comfort, by an arbor of wisteria or of concord grapes. And certainly, as I have proved from direct experience, we will feel much less guilty about our compulsive acquisition of plants and our inability to find an immediate place for them in an already overcrowded garden if they may be stood in an area that is attractive and easy to tend.

Gardeners are not gardeners primarily because they think about the tidiness of their trash cans. Quite the reverse, for it is generally people who do not have the necessities of watering, weeding, deadheading, fertilizing, and simply admiring the garden who have the spiffiest utility areas. But even the most devoted gardeners will find their gardens more beautiful and more satisfying if they look into those odd neglected corners with an eye to how they, also, may be integrated into the garden. For what really makes a garden is the belief that beauty should prevail everywhere, and that no effort is inappropriate to that end, no area unworthy of attention.

Gardening in Small Spaces

A garden is a garden is a garden. That is simply to say that all gardens—large or small, tropical, temperate, or chilly, urban, suburban, or country—reflect, when they are successful, the same fundamental principles of design. Never is that more apparent than in quite small gardens, for although the concepts that guide them will be the same as for any garden, those concepts will have to be even more carefully thought out, even more finely executed. Because of their size, large gardens are very forgiving. As long as one section is splendid, one can turn one's back on others that are resting, or perhaps reflect less than successful experiments. The verges of large gardens can sometimes be ragged, even pleasantly untidy, melting gently into the surrounding woods and fields. But everything in the small garden lies so immediately under the eye that errors of taste or culture loom larger, and excuses for their existence are not so readily available.

As in the making of any garden, the first step in fashioning a small one is to give it a frame by enclosing its space. A firm boundary will paradoxically make that space seem larger, not smaller. Anyone who has ever built a new house will know the panic, standing on its foundation before

135

it is framed, of thinking that the rooms to be are hopelessly small. Once the walls are up, however, the eye is held within boundaries and areas seem more ample. The frame of a small garden—whether of walls, fences, or hedges—has that effect also, concentrating attention on what is within rather than on what is beyond. A strong frame will also give the garden the magic sense of privacy, of a haven, more important perhaps in small gardens than in larger ones, since they are often located in urban or suburban worlds, where what lies beyond may be intrusive. Of course, many small gardens are already enclosed, or partially so, by other buildings and by the neighbors' fences. Where that is so, it is necessary simply to complete the work by constructing frames along the remaining open spaces, bearing always in mind that they will be softened by the addition of vines, espaliers, or shrubs, causing them partially to disappear.

Even when gardens are quite small, they still often benefit by being segmented into rooms, each with its own particular character and purpose, its own emotional resonance. For the same trick of perspective that makes an enclosed space seem larger than an open one makes a divided space seem so, too. It is always hard to know whether the appreciation of a garden is aesthetic or psychological, but in any garden, we love to wander, to explore and discover. Necessarily, however, the techniques used to divide a small garden are different from those employed in larger ones; for whereas large gardens may accommodate tall hedges of yew, internal fences or large masses of shrubbery, the small garden may afford room for only a single shrub, partially masking a quiet seating area, a bench, perhaps, on a pad of stone or brick. Lucky is the owner of a small garden that has an uneven grade, for then a retaining wall with steps let in, or even a single riser of wooden beaming, can signal a change in the garden's mood, endowing it with greater complexity and richness. In the lowest part, there might be a sunken pool, rather formal in character, stone coped and providing a habitat for fascinating aquatic plants, for fish and for the many small creatures—frogs, dragonflies, even turtles—that may find it for themselves. Giving over any part of the small garden to so specialized a purpose will make it seem larger, and certainly more diverting. So above the sunken area there might be a formal herb garden, or one planted to roses, hedged into small beds by boxwoods. Or there could be a series of beds given over to fragrant flowers, or to perennials in a limited range of color, or even to bright annuals for cutting.

Whether changes in grade are possible or not, changes in surfacing are always nice, and in the small garden can subtly differentiate one area from another. An ample path of attractive material—a straight shot or gently curving according to the garden's mood—can serve to section it, leading from the garden gate to the house door, across turf or down to a terraced seating area. In the small garden, a hard-surfaced passage over grass becomes very important, for foot traffic will always traverse the same route, wearing away the turf. Generally, however, owners of small gardens should think hard about their bit of grass, for although a lawn has strong emotional resonances, in small spaces it may be an unaffordable luxury. The smaller a lawn is, the sooner it will be worn down by passage over it, and what was planned as a cool and restful sward will

become a shabby skin of ill grass barely concealing the mud beneath. Turf, also, has the curious quality of reducing space, whereas hard paving expands it. So a very small lawn might make a really ample terrace, one capable of providing room for a bench, several chairs, even a table for outdoor dining. Areas once given over to grass might then become deep beds for perennials and shrubs, some of which might be allowed to tumble over the paved surface. Or, where shade prevails, as, in small gardens, it so often does, hostas might be cultivated, interspersed with ferns and other shade-loving plants, making of the terraced area a cool retreat from urban heat, a sort of oasis.

Probably harder than configuring the space of the small garden is deciding what to grow in it. All gardeners are greedy by definition, and all fight, to a greater or lesser degree, the limits imposed on them. The owners of large gardens, however, always have the luxury of experimentation. If a plant does not do well here, it may be moved there. New ground can be opened for new experiments, new enthusiasms explored. But those who garden in a small space need to be extraordinarily attentive to the circumstances of their site, shaping the garden's character according to its exigencies. If the site is shady, it does no good to crave delphiniums and lilacs, or roses, for they will not flourish, and their sickly, drawn growth will make of the garden not a pleasure but a reproach. Far better in the long run to cultivate the wonderful world of shade plants, many of which will also accept, and even relish, the sour, ill-drained soil common in urban gardens. For in the small garden, everything should be in flourishing good health. Such an effect will require careful selection, some experimentation, and the willingness, when one has done one's best by an ailing plant, to chuck it and choose another.

It goes almost without saying, as well, that one's choices ought to be of the very best plants, the finest varieties. They should be capable not only of growing lustily under the conditions one can provide, but also of paying for their space by providing great interest, usually throughout the year. If one has room for only one tree, then, it might well be a *Stewartia pseudocamelia,* which is graceful in shape, rich with pleated green leaves, bears single, white, camelialike flowers in July, colors brilliantly in autumn, and displays handsome cream, buff, and green-mottled bark in

winter. Although hostas are always satisfying sculptural plants, if space is
very limited it might make more sense to establish instead a clump of
Sasa veitchii, a low-growing bamboo with an equivalent richness of summer foliage but with fascinating buff margination around each leaf all
winter when hostas would have retreated into the bare earth. Deciduous
azaleas are wonderful in May, vivid with flowers of orange, pink, yellow,
or white, but theirs is a brief season, and perhaps *Ilex verticillata,* which
bears its scarlet berries on naked stems all winter long, would provide a
more enduring satisfaction. Or, if one must have an azalea, perhaps it
should be the royal azalea, *Rhododendron schlippenbachii,* for although its
silver-pink blossoms last only a week or two, its autumn color is among
the most brilliant of all deciduous shrubs. Where the most serviceable
ground cover is called for, it might be the white-flowered myrtle
(*Vinca minor* f. *alba*) rather than the blue, or the American pachysandra,
Pachysandra procumbens, instead of the ubiquitous Japanese form,
Pachysandra terminalis.

Whatever the choice of plants may be for the small garden, however,
their range should be limited; and the smaller the garden, the fewer will
be the number of species that should find a home in it. For the newly
escaped apartment dweller in final possession of his own garden, or for
those who move from larger gardens to smaller ones, this is a rule that
will be very hard to follow. Still, the quality of repose, which all gardens
should possess, will depend on avoiding the fiddling effect of growing
one of this, one of that, and some of this other. The smaller the space, the
more the eye will need to rest on ample, extensive masses of plants, and
especially on quiet expanses of foliage. And for those who love plants for
the flowers they produce, an even harder truth to accept may be that in
small gardens, it is leaves, not flowers, that will contribute the greatest
degree of tranquility and repose.

One of the many paradoxes in designing the small garden is that one
must think rather boldly. Nothing should be meager or pinched, for then
the space will become trivial, calling attention to its actual limits. Paths,
then, when they exist, should be broad. Terraces should be as ample as
possible, fences tall enough to guarantee privacy and very sturdy in construction. If pots are to be placed about—and a few pots in a small gar-

den always increase its range and variety—they should be large, possessing the authority of sculpture. Furniture should be solid and commodious. Especially, beds should be as deep as possible, so that the plants in them can be layered three deep at least, partially concealing the frame of the garden and allowing for a play of bays and hollows. But although the range of plants grown in a small garden may be limited, and cultural conditions exacting, it still offers one large benefit. For well-designed, furnished with the choicest plants in flourishing good health, cultivated down to its last square inch of space, a small garden can be a perfect jewel, the envy of those with larger spaces at their command.

Garden Materials

Garden designers are always imagining sites they may some day be called upon to work into beautiful gardens. One of my enduring fantasies is that I will be asked one day to design a garden in the least propitious of all imaginable circumstances. The site I have in mind would be emphatically urban, a small city lot behind a comfortable house with no architectural pretensions, tall and narrow, with the back and front stoop characteristic of many city houses built on spec in the 1920s and 1930s. Around its modest quarter of an acre would be a chain-link fence, beyond which one could catch glimpses of all sorts of urban clutter— parked cars, tangles of telephone wire, a filling station on the opposite corner, perhaps a school (as forbidding as urban schools sadly too often are) a little down the street.

The occupants of this house would be very important to my scheme, as any would-be gardeners who hire a designer must be; for if the garden does not reflect the personality of its owners, it is not a success. I imagine them to be a young couple, both employed, energetic, and imaginative, committed lovers of city life, of concerts and museums and films and cafés, courageous in their acquisition and remodeling of a house in which few could have seen a future. By the time I was called in, the house would have been cleared of generations of wallpaper back to the plaster walls, which would have been freshly painted a pristine white, and the rooms would have been sparingly furnished with a few good modern pieces and several imaginatively restored junk-shop finds. Paintings, prints, and sculpture, quirky and beautiful, would glow against the walls, and the kitchen (which would, of course, be at the back of the house, overlooking the garden to be) would be bright with bare, scrubbed wood and nicely cluttered with shining cookware, with baskets, and with well-thumbed cookbooks. Indoors, all would be beautiful, thought-out, and chosen; outdoors, however, all would be mess and depression, the sort of landscape in which Lizzie Borden might have stood after axing her parents in Fall River, Massachusetts. Neither of my clients would be gardeners; and although firm of taste, neither would have a clue about how to fashion an interesting outdoor space behind their house. Still, they would have needs, probably fairly clearly conceived in their case, but not different, essentially, from the needs of any garden, wherever it is located.

Their first concern would be for privacy, since gardens ought always to be havens, and all profit from some sort of enclosure. In this case, privacy would be an absolute necessity, since what lay beyond, the tangled urban landscape, could hardly be conducive to the tranquility and repose we expect from gardens. They'd surely also like the garden to be an extension of the house, an outdoor room in which they could sit, dine, and entertain guests. Non-gardeners although they are, they would still like plants that possessed some intrinsic interest, functioning almost as pieces of sculpture, worth studying in themselves (and learning their Latin names) as forms and shapes. With little time to fiddle in the garden, and little interest (as yet) they'd want a landscape that gave much and asked little. Finally—and especially in their case—they would want a clear style, something beyond the predictable, something that quickened their aesthetic eye and reflected the same principles of quirky good taste that had shaped their internal environment. Such givens, clearly expressed, are as rich with possibilities as the site I imagine is deficient. They suggest a clear intention, a guiding vision with which every choice of plant or material must be in accord.

The chain-link fence must be accepted for what it is, a firm barrier in so narrow a space and a necessary security precaution. Although such a thing must be the despair of many gardeners who own one, chain link is not a hopeless material against which to work. The trick, in this case, would be to make it seem a choice rather than an intractable given. So I think I might extend it in an arm across the back of the space, subdivid-

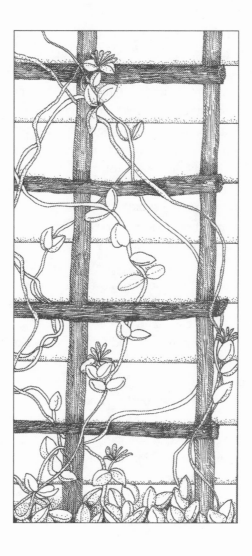

ing the ground by roughly a third, leaving room for an entrance to the right side. I might also choose to extend the chain link upward, into an arbor over this third, over which grapes or perhaps ampelopsis or Virginia creeper could be trained to provide a shady seating area, perhaps even an outdoor dining room. That would leave me with the problem of concealing or softening the two boundary sides, which could be done with many vines or evergreen shrubs, but which in this case might be most wonderfully achieved by a tall bamboo, probably *Phyllostachys aureosulcata,* which, if firmly held from spreading within by a three-foot barrier of metal buried in the earth, would feather thickly against the fence, providing privacy and moving with each rare breeze.

Grass, in so small a space, would be out of the question, and so some paving should cover the ground, leaving only a narrow strip along its edges for softening plantings. The choice of paving should be very careful, for it should not look too polished, too expensive, too discordant with the asphalt streets beyond and the cement sidewalks. Brick, then, would probably be ruled out, as would sophisticated pavers of thick bluestone. Fieldstone would be costly, and would suggest just the sort of rural cottage charm I would be straining to avoid. Some material long associated with urban landscapes would be desirable, and so I might choose granite cobbles, thousands of which underlie city streets beneath the asphalt, or even irregular pieces of broken cement sidewalk, laid in a pattern of crazy pavement. Whichever choice I settled on, I would want the pavement to be laid on sand, so that grasses, weeds, and desirable plants might come to colonize its edges and even extend into the middle where foot traffic was not too great. With my paving, I would fashion a broad terrace below the back stoop and the kitchen door, leaving three feet or so on either side against my bamboo hedge, and a wider bed against the chain-link trellis at the back, traversed by a three-foot path of the same material. All these beds might be planted with bright perennials and annuals (and some should certainly be included, in spontaneous-seeming drifts) but the primary plantings would be of ornamental grasses, tall miscanthus in several species and varieties, silvery-blue helichtotrichons and fescues, with, here and there (used very sparingly), a broad-leaved perennial—a hosta, a bergenia, or a *Sedum spectabile* 'Autumn Joy'—included for accent and for

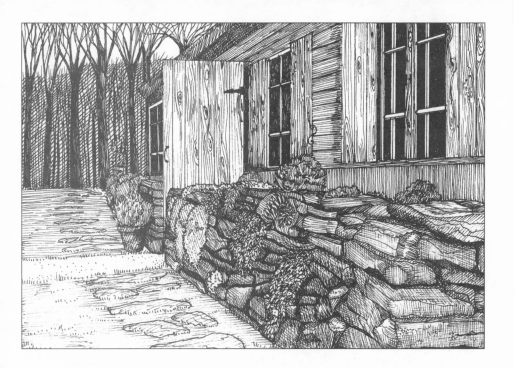

depth. What I would be trying to achieve would be an effect similar to urban weeds, and so nothing should seem overly patterned or contrived. To vary the texture of the bamboo, I might not even shrink from planting *Polygonum cuspidatum,* the rampant Japanese "knot weed," against the back portion of the chain-link fence.

The greatest fun I would have with this garden—still an imaginary one—would be in its container plantings. For plants in pots, tubs, and urns are always a feature of urban gardens, and tend, in small spaces, to increase complexity and enlarge the space. In this case, however, I would mostly avoid expensive and sophisticated planters and pots, whether of good Italian terra rosa or suave boxes like Caisses de Versailles. Rather, I would consider what could be done with galvanized garbage cans, a little beat-up if possible, oxidized, and cut down to interesting shapes. In them I might plant other grasses, or perhaps in one, a collection of culinary herbs, basil and oregano and sage and chives. Where a really strong feature was needed, I might consider a dwarf evergreen, an Alberta spruce, or a golden, thread-leaved chamaecyparis. All of these pots I would stage carefully throughout the garden, by twos and threes of varying heights, or singly, at corners of the terrace or at the juncture of the path leading to the arbor. Whether what is called a "water feature" would be nice is in doubt. It would depend on where I could tuck it, half lost in overhanging grasses or bamboos. But if one were included, it should be still, not a fountain that seemed as if someone had forgotten to jiggle the toilet handle. It might be of the same cobble work as the pavement, or of broken cement, but it could as well be a galvanized tank for watering horses, which come in graceful, oval shapes, fluted and of the same material as garbage cans. In it would be a few goldfish, to eliminate mosquitos, and some submerged pots of cyperus, or hardy rushes. If there could be a skin of duckweed across the water, so much the better.

This fantasy garden exists (so far) only in my mind, but it illustrates many of the points that must be made about choosing garden materials. The first is that they should always be harmonious with the general intent or idea of the garden. If it is urban, then it is worth considering with fresh eyes materials that are associated with the urban landscape. If it is rural, conversely, then one must look around for materials native to the place, to split locust or other farm fences, to stone walls, pavers of good flat local fieldstone, and to the indigenous architecture of sheds, barns, and outbuildings. Sophisticated city gardens, such as exist behind fine Georgian town houses, will call for terraces and paths of wide slabbed bluestone, or for brick, bordered by clipped hedges of box and framed with trim walls of yew. Gardens of ample extent, whether suburban or rural, seem always to demand quiet expanses of lawn, bordered by generous beds of deciduous and evergreen shrubs. Simple cottages may be crowded with flowers and even vegetables up to the door, but such abundance might seem trivial and cluttered before a stately Victorian mansion, where a foundation planting of evergreens, a simple ground cover, and a single specimen of deciduous magnolia would be better. Rock gardens are best made by those who have a deep knowledge of rare rock plants and who long to grow them in the habitat to which they are suited, but even then, many rock gardens can seem carbuncles on the ground unless the terrain is suitably sloped and distant mountains validate the man-made outcroppings of granite against which dianthus and androsaces hover.

In all these cases, perhaps no greater garden wisdom exists than that voiced by Alexander Pope, that one must first consider "the genius of the place." From a full understanding of one's site, its conditions and its peculiar resonances, will follow a multitude of choices, of plants and materials, of framing devices, of pavement and individual features. Such elements must necessarily respond—one would say resonate—to the greater surroundings beyond the garden, or to the greater spirit of gardening as it has been practiced, however imperfectly, in that place.

That is a first principle, but in the making of a garden, it is not necessarily the last. For gardeners are willful people, and of all the arts, perhaps gardening is the only one that smiles on plagiarism, and that lends itself to the recreation of whatever the gardener fancies. Hardly a one of the specific descriptions offered here could not be bent, even violated, in the creation of a garden, perhaps a garden of great beauty. Probably the general theories, however—the great abstractions that control successful gardening, of intention and frame—should never be ignored. But once a garden space has been defined firmly by some surround, whether fence or wall, hedge or loose groupings of shrubs, and once the gardener has seized on some central guiding idea or intention, everything else should proceed, resulting in the perfect harmony that is a good garden.

Wood to Garden

*F*or too many of us, when we think of gardening we think of a trip to the garden center. Especially in springtime, the allure of ever so many smug little PJM rhododendrons, potently budded forsythias, and neatly balled French lilacs, all standing out in serried ranks in the nursery yard, is too much to resist. The winter, after all, has been long and gray and—to say the least—short on flowers. So we buy what we see, as many as our wallet can afford and our car or truck accommodate. We take them home and plant them.

The sense that something is wrong occurs late or soon, but it surely occurs. This is not, after all, the first time we have given in to our craving for bright flowers. Last year we also bought the PJMs, and planted them near the forsythia. This year we have bought a crab apple as well, straight of trunk and nicely branched, with little nosegays of bright red buds already nestled in rosettes of tender green leaves up and down its stems. Perhaps we could plant it in the front lawn?

Of course, what is wrong here is more than the unwillingness of a chrome-yellow forsythia to look good next to an orchid-pink rhododendron, or the impossibility that both should sympathize with the crab apple's foam of carmine pink. What is wrong is our whole approach to gardening, especially in spring, making of its passing almost a relief and teaching us yet again that the irresistible urge to go out and buy some bushes is not the way to make a garden.

Gardens are idealized landscapes. At their best, the shapes and colors of their plants, and especially the arrangement of their spaces, should make them seem refinements of the natural world that lies around them.

And very often, the desire to create a garden can best be realized not by planting exotic garden-center offerings here and there about the place, but by purifying what nature has already planted.

To live in the country is to live in or near the woods. Once, all of New England was shaded by a dense primeval forest, which European settlers systematically cleared to build their houses and ships, but more often simply to create rich pastures for grazing and fields for the raising of agricultural crops. By the beginning of this century, it is estimated that only 10 percent of Vermont and New Hampshire remained wooded, and out of the demise of the ancient forest was built a thriving economy of sheep, dairy, and trucking farms. The development of the railways, and later of the highway system, dramatically reversed this pattern, causing a shift of agriculture first to the Midwest and then to the West. The thrifty farms of New England were abandoned, and their fertile, patiently stoned fields were repossessed by the forest, leaving the old stone walls to thread neglected through the woods.

The newly regrown eastern American forest, hardly fifty or even thirty years of age, is a marvelously varied plant community, more abundant by far in diverse species than was the original primeval woods. It includes the great evergreen white pines and hemlocks, firs and spruces, the noble deciduous beeches, maples, oaks, yellow woods, and tulip trees, and a rich and complex understory of smaller leaf-losing trees and shrubs, shadblow, dogwood, witch hazel, moose wood, and leather wood. In the central reaches of New England, broad-leaved ericaceous shrubs, laurel and rhododendron, add permanent weight and magnificent flower to the shadows of the great trees. South of Boston grows the incomparable American holly, *Ilex opaca,* its dull-green leaves and sparkling berries far more beautiful and serene than its celebrated English counterpart. In the wetter places, often the work of beavers, grows another holly, the deciduous *Ilex verticillata,* called "Sparkleberry" for its sprays of scarlet fruit most apparent in late autumn when it has shed its leaves. Close to it one can often find tall specimens of high-bush blueberry, more precious for its gnarled and contorted structure, its fragrant white bells in spring and its vivid autumn coloration even than for its delicious summer-born fruit. And beneath all this richness of greater and lesser trees and shrubs, evergreen or autumn colored, is a marvelously beautiful flora of fern and wood-loving perennial and rare orchid. Here, in all this, is the stuff of which to make a splendid garden.

But the forests of New England are still new forests, second or third growth, far from the serene and moving quiet of the climax old-growth forest we can now only imagine. Time alone can bring again what our forests once were, great ages of time far longer than the life spans of the youngest among us. But we can, with artful shaping and discrete replanting, achieve an echo of that great forest, and, with what we have, we can weave a texture of greater variety and complexity than what once was, thereby satisfying every gardener's urge to have some of everything. We can, in other words, make a garden of our woods.

The first step in making a garden of the woods is an act difficult for most who love plants. It is to kill a great many of them. Trees must be cut down, often without regard for the claims any might have on our affections. Although one might with luck inherit a fine old sugar bush into which, through neglect, a few trees other than maples have crept, or a woodlot that has been under the management of a woodsman with an eye as keen for aesthetics as for utility, the obvious fact about much of the great Eastern forest is that it has grown up much too thickly. It is, in the picturesque Yankee word, "scrub."

To bring into being the woodland garden we envision, we must therefore thin the woods, removing sometimes as much as two thirds of its standing timber. What we want is a forest in which the trunks of the trees stand generally not less than thirty feet from one another. This is first to give each of the remaining trees sufficient freedom from competition for light, air, and nutrients so that it can begin to swell and grow into a magnificent representative of its species. Such spacing also allows light to fall into and through the trees to the forest floor below. Little will grow, and less will grow well, in the black shade of a thick forest canopy. Almost all woodland plants want shifting, dappled shade to flourish.

Of course, this thirty feet of distance is only a rule of thumb, and one to be rather freely interpreted. Sometimes, to vary the patterning of the woods and avoid monotony, trees should be left to stand as a pair or trio quite close together, forming one single crown with two or three trunks.

Sometimes, also, a particularly fine tree or group of trees should be set apart at greater distance so that the light falls all around, highlighting their beauty. And here and there about the woods, open clearings must be left in such a way as to allow shafts of sunlight to fall unimpeded to the forest floor. Such clearings will not only allow a few precious sun lovers to grow, they will also draw the eye through the woods from clearing to clearing, for there is nothing more magical than the beckoning of light in deep, leafy shade.

In woodland "management," what has traditionally been sought is economic utility. It has been said, perhaps with exaggeration, that the only trees a hundred years old in New England are sugar maples, because they produced a steady crop and even when they were not tapped they were left because someone might "get around to it" someday. Otherwise, trees of all other species have been harvested, the great oaks and ageless pines for beams and flooring, the basswoods and birches for easily worked cabinet wood, the stately black locusts for rot-resistant fencing, and the clean, straight ashes for ax handles to fell more forest. Diseased or moribund trees were taken for firewood, leaving only the young trees behind for the next cash crop. But in the making of a woodland garden, we seek an end other than economic utility. For one thing, we want to encourage species diversity, not uniformity, both because the resulting woodland is more beautiful and also because it is healthier. Nothing so encourages disease and insect predation as large stands of one species only. So we must leave representatives of those species that would be taken for their value by woodland managers, such as a stately oak or a well-grown ash; we must also leave the "junk" trees, the shapely little hemlocks and the beautiful spindly moosewood, *Acer pennsylvanicum,* that never comes to any account economically but that gladdens us in winter with its green-striped bark and in summer with its wide palmate leaves. In this way, our woodland becomes a microcosm of nature, as a garden should be, reflecting her rich diversity.

Another place where we must part company with traditional woodlot practices is in our attitude to the dead and dying. Aged and decaying trees are rich in food, for insects and thus for birds. They provide crucial nesting places for some of our most cherished summer visitors, bluebirds among them. And you will never hear the raucous laughter of the woodpeckers or their rapid-fire hammering unless you leave an ancient, decaying skag of beech deep in the woods. Besides, a great old hulk of tree, miraculously alive despite decay and prepared still to last your life or mine, contributes grandly to the sense of aged nature that is the spiritual heart of a woodland garden.

But the thinning of the forest is not all there is to making it a garden. Gardens are nature idealized, so we will almost certainly want to enrich the naturally occurring flora, to plant what might have grown just in that spot but has not. Whether to plant only native plants or to allow "exotics" depends in part on the kind of garden the gardener envisions. but it also depends on our definition of what is meant by "native." To the strictest conservationists, native plants, and no others, are those that occur on a particular plot of land. Broader interpretations allow plants native to a particular ecosystem, a state or region or climatic zone, and include plants that would once have grown in a particular place and still exist elsewhere, nearby or perhaps in similar conditions far away. The inclusion of some of these plants in one's own woodland is actually a gesture of conservation, for it establishes seed colonies in places where the plant can be expected to thrive in replacement of its own particular habitat, which may be endangered.

But however one defines the concept, few gardeners will be content with what occurs naturally on the site. Sooner or later one's eye will be caught by a thriving clump of trillium down the road, growing in just the conditions one can offer at home, or by a vivid pinxter bloom flourishing in an abandoned acid pasture whose owner, for a small price, may be approachable. Here, however, the strongest word of caution must be given to anyone who loves the natural world and seeks to recreate it. For no matter how confident one may be of one's skills at transplanting, and no matter how abundant a stand of wildflowers may be, taking them from naturally occurring stands reduces by just so much their capacity to continue in the wild. One may not be the only one, after all, who noticed that bank of trailing arbutus or maidenhair fern, nor the only one whose conscience lost the battle to one's love of beauty. The digging of flowers from the wild is a crime, both actually in the case of the greater and

greater number of endangered species, and spiritually when it reduces the heritage of us all. Despite the impressive efforts of conservationists, however, ours is still an expanding nation, and very often the accumulating of native plants by skilled gardeners is a moral act when the alternative is their loss through the widening of roads and the bulldozing of woodland for new homes. Permission can usually be secured from the foreman of the road crew or from a developer to collect what would otherwise be lost, providing one is willing to dig early in the morning or after the crews have quit working so as not to be in the way. Failing such opportunities, however, one should restrict one's acquisitions to the many small mail-order nurseries that are able to certify that their stock is not collected from the wild, or to the many native species that are cutting-grown by large nurseries from their own stock plants. A third source of native plants, and the best of all, is nature herself. For once a proper habitat has been prepared, many wild plants will return spontaneously to the places they once grew.

The concept of the woodland garden, however, is as much an aesthetic as a biological one. Many species that are not, in fact, native to North

America can be beautiful in the woodland garden if used with tact. They can also make possible effects the gardener could not otherwise achieve. For example, nature often clothes the trunks of trees with vines. But save one splendid example, *Parthenocissus virginiana,* the lovely Virginia creeper that paints the forest scarlet in September a week or so before the trees themselves show color, the New England woodland is short on vines, and others must be added. None, perhaps, could be better than the climbing Hydrangea, *Hydrangea anomala petiolaris.* It thrives in close competition with deciduous trees and can clothe the trunk of the tallest maple almost to the top. Bare of leaves, its thick, woody stems are beautiful in winter, and its loose, light corymbs of white flower produced in early summer seem to accord perfectly with the cool forest shade.

One fascinating way of introducing exotic plants to a natural garden is to plant congeners. These are plants from places other than North Amer-

ica—Japan, China, Northern Europe—that are close cousins of native plants, sprung from a common ancestor but following a different evolutionary path after the breakup of the great continental plates. So our native jack-in-the-pulpit, *Arisaema triphyllum,* has in a Japanese counterpart, *A. ringens,* with flowers rather like snails in shape, and in its meltingly beautiful white Chinese cousin, *A. candidissimum,* congeners that seem wholly right in the New England woods. Congeners exist in every class of plants from tall trees to fragile forest-floor perennials and ferns. There are Asiatic maples and birches, the European beech in many forms, Chinese hollies and Asiatic witch hazels. One of my favorites is a congener to our own very fine bog arum, the yellow-flowered *Lysichiton Americanum; L. camtschatcense,* from Siberia, closely resembles it, but bears spathes of stunning white.

Still, what must be avoided in the woodland garden is the creation of a kind of horticultural bazaar crammed with all kinds of odd and unusual plants just because they will live in the woodland garden or because we like them for themselves. The harmony that is obtained by limiting the palette to native plants (assuming that we do not define that term too narrowly) is an enormously useful aesthetic lesson. Although an occasional exotic species may be introduced to do the work for which we have no native plants, or because in form and color it resonates with the native flora, still, the woodland garden must never seem anything but the labor of a beneficent nature, however responsible the gardener may be for its shaping.

More than any other single element, however, more even than the selecting of trees or the planting of new ones, it is the path through the woodland garden that will influence the experience of its viewers. To begin with, there must of course *be* a path, for however small it is, a woods one cannot wander through is as pointless and frustrating as a lawn one cannot walk on. So crucial are paths to our experience of gardens that we notice them immediately, long before we notice other elements, even major trees or large rocks or magnificent stands of flower. Paths are to the garden what a plot is to a novel, controlling our experience in something of the same way by guiding us through the garden's intricacies and unfolding its "episodes." In a garden, only water is more prominent than a path, and a path leading to water can often be garden enough. But in the woodland garden, which lacks the formal structures of hedge and bed line, paths are all the more crucial, as they give subtle form and meaning to what must still seem like spontaneous shapes and masses.

The most beautiful paths are always the paths of least resistance, born of the simple need to get from here to there as easily and quietly as possible. All animals, wild and domestic, know better than the gardener often does how to make a path. Cows, particularly, are geniuses at this art, and the paths they make are never straight and tedious, but curve gracefully to avoid an obstacle, such as a large rock or fallen tree, and hug the valleys to disappear in the easiest way around a hill. They are studies in deep purpose, and the gardener who has such natural paths should deviate from them only for the best and surest reasons. Failing the wisdom of the animals, it is good advice to put in no path until the space has been walked many times. In the matter of paths, one's feet sometimes think better than one's head, and the paths they form will often look better than those born of conscious attempt.

And all paths must lead somewhere, for there is nothing more frustrating in a garden than a blank dead end that forces one to turn back and re-traverse the ground without refreshment. Of all rewards, probably none is better at the end of a path than a seat or bench, not necessarily because one may be tired, but more because the stationary experience of viewing a garden is quite different from the ambulatory one. In a woodland garden, some resting place along the path or at its end is all the more important, for the magical play of light through the trees, the rustle of small creatures and the song of birds, the subtle beauty of leaves and sunlit trunks, are most apparent when one is still, and can sit and stare.

Index